Amgen : Broken

By/Gan **Gary Owen**

This play was produced by Sherman Cymru and first performed at Sherman, Cardiff, on Friday 1 May, 2009.
Cynhyrchwyd y ddrama hon gan Sherman Cymru, a'i pherfformio gyntaf yn Sherman, Caerdydd ar Ddydd Gwener 1 Mai, 2009.

Cover Image/*Delwedd y Clawr*: Kirsten McTernan
Design/*Dylunio*: Rhys Huws
Typesetting/*Cysodwyd gan*: Eira Fenn

Printed in Wales by Cambrian Printers, Aberystwyth. This book is published with the financial support of the Welsh Books Council.
Argraffwyd yng Nghymru gan Wasg Cambrian, Aberystwyth. Cyhoeddir y llyfr hwn gyda chefnogaeth ariannol Cyngor Llyfrau Cymru.

ISBN: 0-9551466-7-4
978-0-9551466-7-1

CAST/CAST

Gary	Steven Meo
Gareth	Simon Watts

PRODUCTION TEAM/TÎM CYNHYRCHU

Writer/Awdur	Gary Owen
Director/Cyfarwyddwr	Elen Bowman
Designer/Cynllunydd	Naomi Dawson
Lighting Designer/ Cynllunydd Goleuo	Katharine Williams
Music and Sound/ Cerddoriaeth a Sain	Simon Allen
Sound Associate/Cysylltydd Sain	Gareth Evans
Movement Director/ Cyfarwyddwr Symud	Liz Ranken
Stage Manager/ Rheolwr Llwyfan	Ben Tyreman
Deputy Stage Manager/ Dirprwy Reolwr Llwyfan	Rachel Burgess
Assistant Directors/ Cyfarwyddwyr Cynorthwyol	Sarah Bickerton Sita Calvert-Ennals Bridget Keehan

THANKS/DIOLCHIADAU

Cardiff University Students' Union; Cardiff & Vale Mental Health Service; Whitchurch Hospital; Amy Johnson; Angharad Griffin; Matthew Gravelle; Sion Pritchard; Rhydian Jones; Simon Neehan; Dominic Leclurc.

SHERMAN CYMRU

We aim to make and present great theatre that is ambitious, inventive and memorable for our audiences, and to create strong, responsive and enriching relationships with our communities. We strive to create the best theatre we can; to achieve a distinct and diverse programme for our audiences; to engage our communities in the creative process of theatre making; and to make a lasting contribution to the national and international development of theatre in Wales. We produce work in both English and Welsh, and tour widely within Wales and the UK.

To be kept in touch about Sherman Cymru events register for our e-bulletin online at **www.shermancymru.co.uk**

Capital Newsflash……
Sherman Cymru is getting ever closer to the much needed redevelopment and refurbishment of the building. By the time you read this, we should have heard from the Arts Council of Wales if our application for a Capital Grant to cover 75% of the total cost has been successful. If it has been the decision will be a real landmark for us and will mean we can move confidently forward into the next phase of a process that will transform our audience's experience of the building and enhance backstage areas for staff and participants. We still need to raise £1.5 million, and will need your help to achieve this. News about how you can get involved can be found at: **www.shermancymru.co.uk/capital**

Sherman Cymru acknowledges the public investment of the Arts Council of Wales and Cardiff Council without whose support our work could not continue. Our Learning and Engagement work i s currently supported by Barclays, Arts & Business Cymru, Paul Hamlyn Foundation and The Rayne Foundation. Recent productions and projects have also been supported by Esmée Fairbairn Foundation, Oakdale Trust and The Peggy Ramsay Foundation.

SHERMAN CYMRU

Ein nod yw cynhyrchu a chyflwyno theatr uchelgeisiol, dyfeisgar a chofiadwy ar gyfer ein cynulleidfaoedd, ac i greu cysylltiadau cryf, ymatebol a chyfoethog gyda'n cymunedau. Yn ganolog i'r gwaith mae ein hymrwymiad i greu'r theatr gorau posibl; i ddarparu rhaglen unigryw ac amrywiol i'n cynulleidfaoedd; i ymgysylltu â'n cymunedau yn y broses greadigol o greu theatr; ac i wneud cyfraniad parhaol i ddatblygiad cenedlaethol a rhyngwladol y theatr yng Nghymru. Rydyn ni'n cynhyrchu gwaith Saesneg a Chymraeg ac yn teithio'n helaeth o amgylch Cymru a'r DU.

Am fwy o wybodaeth am weithgareddau Sherman Cymru ac i gofrestru ar gyfer ein e-fwletin ewch i **www.shermancymru.co.uk**

Newyddion Cyfalaf......
Mae Sherman Cymru yn agosáu eto fyth tuag at y gwaith gwbl angenrheidiol o ailddatblygu ac adnewyddu'r adeilad. Erbyn i chi ddarllen hwn dylem fod wedi clywed gan Gyngor Celfyddydau Cymru os yw ein cais am Grant Cyfalaf, i gyflenwi 75% o'r gost, wedi bod yn llwyddiannus. Byddai dyfarniad cadarnhaol yn garreg filltir i ni fel cwmni, ac yn golygu y gallwn symud ymlaen yn hyderus tuag at y cam nesaf yn y broses - proses fydd yn trawsffurfio profiad ein cynulleidfa o'r adeilad ac a fydd yn gwella'r ardaloedd cefn llwyfan i staff a chyfranogwyr. Byddwn dal angen codi £1.5 miliwn, a bydd angen eich cymorth chi i gyflawni hyn. Gallwch weld sut i chwarae eich rhan drwy edrych ar: **www.shermancymru.co.uk/cyfalaf**

Mae Sherman Cymru yn cydnabod buddsoddiad cyhoeddus Cyngor Celfyddydau Cymru a Chyngor Caerdydd. Ni fyddai'n bosib i ni barhau â'n gwaith heb eu cefnogaeth. Ar hyn o bryd cefnogir ein gwaith Dysg ac Ymgysylltu gan Barclays, Arts & Business Cymru, Sefydliad Paul Hamlyn a Sefydliad Rayne. Mae rhai o'n cynyrchiadau diweddar hefyd wedi derbyn cefnogaeth gan Sefydliad Esmée Fairbairn, Ymddiriedolaeth Oakdale a Sefydliad Peggy Ramsay.

SHERMAN CYMRU STAFF/STAFF SHERMAN CYMRU

Director/Cyfarwyddwr
Chris Ricketts

General Manager/Rheolwr Cyffredinol
Margaret Jones

Associate Directors/ Cyfarwyddwyr Cyswllt
Arwel Gruffydd
Amy Hodge

Artistic Associate/Cyswllt Artistig
Elen Bowman

Artistic Coordinator/Cyd-lynydd Artistig
Kate Perridge

Literary Manager/Rheolwr Llenyddol
Sian Summers

Literary Assistant/Cynorthwy-ydd Llenyddol
Branwen Davies

Administrator/Gweinyddwr
Elin Partridge

DEVELOPMENT/DATBLYGU

Head of Development/Pennaeth Datblygu
Emma Goad

FINANCE/CYLLID

Head of Finance/Pennaeth Cyllid
Michael Gowing

Finance Assistant/Cynorthwy-ydd Cyllid
Marion Price

LEARNING & ENGAGEMENT/ DYSG AC YMGYSYLLTU

Head of Learning & Engagement/ Pennaeth Dysg ac Ymgysylltu
Jess Naish

Director, Youth Theatre & New Artists Development/Cyfarwyddwr, Theatr Ieuenctid a Datblygiad Artistiaid Newydd
Phillip Mackenzie

Acting Out Cardiff Coordinator/ Cyd-lynydd Acting Out Caerdydd
Jason Camilleri

Directors, Community Enagagement/Cyfarwyddwyr, Ymrwymiad â'r Gymuned
Jason Camilleri, Llinos Mai

Learning & Engagement Assistant/Cynorthwy-ydd Dysg ac Ymgysylltu
Heather Jones

MARKETING & CUSTOMER RELATIONS/MARCHNATA A CHYSYLLTIADAU CWSMERIAID

Head of Marketing & Customer Relations/Pennaeth Marchnata a Chysylltiadau
Haleh Tozer

Marketing & Campaigns Manager/ Rheolwr Marchnata ac Ymgyrchu
Suzanne Carter

Media & Marketing Officer/ Swyddog Cyfryngau a Marchnata
Jenny Boyatt

Marketing Officer/ Swyddog Marchnata
Bethan Way

Box Office Manager/ Rheolwr y Swyddfa Docynnau
Laura Brayford

Box Office Assistants/ Cynorthwy-wyr y Swyddfa Docynnau, Jane Allison
Alison King, Rachel McGrath

House Manager/ Rheolwr Tŷ
Marina Newth

PRODUCTIONS & OPERATIONS/CYNHYRCHU A GWEITHREDIADAU

Head of Production & Operations/Pennaeth Cynhyrchu a Gweithrediadau
Nick Allsop

Chief Electrician/Prif Drydanwr
Rachel Mortimer

Deputy Chief Electrician/Is Brif Drydanwr
Katy Stephenson

Deputy Chief Electrician (Sound)/Is Brif Drydanwr(Sain)
Gareth Evans

Technical Stage Manager/ Rheolwr Llwyfan Technegol
Gareth Gordon

Wardrobe Manager/Rheolwr Gwisgoedd
Deryn Tudor

Stage Door Receptionists/ Derbynyddion Drws y Llwyfan
Jane Allison, Helen Beveridge
Iain Goosey, Anna Harris
Glenn Jones, Brenda Knight
Ceri Mill

Steven Meo
Gary

Steven trained at the Royal Welsh College of Music and Drama. He is an Associate Artist at Clwyd Theatr Cymru.
Hyfforddwyd Steven yng Ngholeg Brenhinol Cerdd a Drama Cymru. Mae e'n Artist Cyswllt gyda Clwyd Theatr Cymru.

Theatre/Theatr
Includes/*Yn cynnwys*: *Great Expectations*, *Under Milk Wood*, *Portrait of the Artist as a Young Dog*, *Dealer's Choice* (Clwyd Theatr Cymru); *Woyzeck* (Wyeside Theatre); *East from the Gantry* (Edinburgh Festival); *Metamorphosis* (Merlin Theatre, Budapest); *Up'n'Under* (Bristol Old Vic); *Flesh and Blood* (Sherman Theatre Company); *Crazy Gary's Mobile Disco* (Paines Plough/ Lyric Hammersmith); *Beautiful Thing* (Sound Theatre).

Television/Teledu
Includes/*Yn cynnwys*: *Nice Girl*, *Score*, *Belonging*, *Holby City*, *High Hopes*, *Roger Roger*, *Innovations*, *The Trouble with George*, *Doctors*, *Spine Chillers*, *Torchwood*, *Grown Ups*, *Casualty*, *Uncle Mike* (BBC Television); *Without Motive*, *Good Arrows* (ITV).

Radio/Radio
Under Milk Wood, *Honey*, *Fallen*, *The Owl Service*, *Cube of the Rainbow*, *The Harbour*, *In Parenthesis* (BBC Radio).

Simon Watts
Gareth

Simon trained at the Rose Bruford College, London.
Hyfforddwyd Simon yng Ngholeg Rose Bruford, Llundain.

Theatre/Theatr
Includes/*Yn cynnwys*: *Great Expectations*, *Drowned Out*, *A Midsummer Night's Dream*, *To Kill a Mockingbird*, *Flora's War* (Clwyd Theatr Cymru); *Porth y Byddar* (Clwyd Theatr Cymru/Theatr Genedlaethol Cymru); *Cysgod y Cryman* (Theatr Genedlaethol Cymru); *Julius Caesar*, *Two Gentlemen of Verona* (Royal Shakespeare Company); *The Happiest Days of Your Life* (Royal Exchange, Manchester); *Cressida* (Almeida Theatre); *Accrington Pals*, *Under Milk Wood*, *Charlotte's Web*, *A Christmas Carol* (Dukes Theatre, Lancaster); *A Midsummer Night's Dream* (Wimbledon Theatre, London); *Bouncers* (Crowne Plaze, Dubai); *The Hobbit* (UK tour).

Television/Teledu
Call on Her, *Rocket Man*, *William Jones* (BBC Television); *Y Pris* (Fiction Factory); *Treflan* (S4C).

Film/Ffilm
The Journey Home (Working Title); *Bronnau Meddwi Caru* (Opus); *Y Mapiwr* (Ffilmiau Gaucho).

Radio/Radio
Doctor Who (BBC Worldwide); *New Adverntures of Bernice Summerfield* (Big Finish).

Gary Owen
Writer/Awdur

Gary's work has been translated into a dozen languages and performed all over the world. In the UK, he has been commissioned by the Royal National Theatre, the National Theatre of Scotland, Hampstead Theatre, Paines Plough, Sherman Cymru, Clwyd Theatr Cymru and the Palace Theatre, Watford.
Mae gwaith Gary wedi ei gyfieithu i ddwsin o ieithoedd ac wedi ei berfformio ar draws y byd. Yn y DU, fe'i gomisiynwyd gan Royal National Theatre, National Theatre of Scotland, Hampstead Theatre, Paines Plough, Sherman Cymru, Clwyd Theatr Cymru a'r Palace Theatre, Watford.

His plays include/*Mae ei ddramâu yn cynnwys*: *Crazy Gary's Mobile Disco, The Shadow of a Boy, The Drowned World, Ghost City.*

His plays have won the George Devine Award, the Meyer Whitworth Award, the Pearson Best Play Award and a Fringe First at the Edinburgh Festival.
Mae ei ddramâu wedi ennill gwobrau George Devine, Meyer Whitworth, Pearson Best Play a Fringe First yng Ngŵyl Caeredin.

Elen Bowman
Director/Cyfarwyddwr

Elen trained at RADA and the School of the Science of Acting. Elen is an an Artistic Associate at Sherman Cymru.
Hyfforddwyd Elen yn RADA ac Ysgol 'The Science of Acting'. *Mae Elen yn Gyswllt Artistig gyda Sherman Cymru.*

Theatre/Theatr
As Director/*Fel Cyfarwyddwr*: Elen has worked with companies including Method & Madness, Bristol Old Vic and Sgript Cymru. In 1999, Elen formed Living Pictures Productions with her partner Robert Bowman - the company specialises in professional development for directors in Cardiff and London. Elen is also a freelance TV and Film Director.
Mae Elen wedi gweithio gyda chwmnïau yn cynnwys Method & Madness, Bristol Old Vic a Sgript Cymru. Ym 1999 sefydlodd Elen Living Pictures Productions gyda'i phartner Robert Bowman - mae'r cwmni yn arbenigo mewn datblygiad proffesiynol i gyfarwyddwyr yng Nghaerdydd a Llundain. Mae Elen hefyd yn gyfarwyddwr teledu a ffilm ar ei liwt ei hun.

Naomi Dawson
Designer/Cynllunydd

Naomi trained at Wimbledon School of Art and Kunstacademie, Maastricht. She is part of the artists' collective SpRoUt, recently exhibiting in Galerija SC, Zagreb.
Hyfforddwyd Naomi yn y Wimbledon School of Art a'r Kunstacademie, Maastricht. Mae hi'n aelod o'r gydweithfa artistiaid SpRoUt ac wedi arddangos ei gwaith yn ddiweddar yn Galerija SC, Zagreb.

Theatre/Theatr
Includes/*Yn cynnwys: King Pelican, Speed Death of the Radiant Child* (Drum Theatre, Plymouth); *...Sisters* (Gate/Headlong); *State of Emergency, Mariana Pineda* (Gate); *Can Any Mother Help Me?* (Courtyard, Hereford); *The Container* (Underbelly, Edinburgh); *Stallerhof, Richard III, The Cherry Orchard, Summer Begins* (Southwark Playhouse); *Phaedra's Love* (Barbican Pit/Bristol Old Vic); *Different Perspectives* (Contact Theatre, Manchester); *Senora Carrar's Rifles, The Pope's Wedding, Forest of Thorns* (Young Vic Studio); *Market Tales* (Unicorn); *Attempts On Her Life, Widows* (BAC); *In Blood, Venezuela, Mud, Trash, Headstone* (Arcola Theatre); *Pass the Parcel* (Theatre Royal, Stratford); *A Thought in Three Parts* (Burton Taylor).

Film/Ffilm
Credits include/*Gwaith yn cynnwys*: Costume Design for the short film *Love After a Fashion* and Set Design for *Fragile* by Idris Khan.
Cynllunio Gwisgoedd ar gyfer y ffilm fer Love After a Fashion a Chynllunio Set ar gyfer Fragile gan Idris Khan.

Katharine Williams
Lighting Designer/
Cynllunydd Goleuo

Katharine has worked as a lighting designer for drama, dance, physical theatre and opera, both within UK and internationally.
Mae Katharine wedi gweithio fel cynllunydd goleuo ar gyfer drama, dawns, theatr gorfforol ac opera, o fewn y DU ac yn rhyngwladol.

Recent designs include/
Mae cynlluniau diweddar yn cynnwys: *Faeries* (Royal Opera House); *Outré* (Darren Johnston, Italy/*Yr Eidal*); *Collaborators Exhibition* (V&A Museum); *Our Country's Good* (Watermill, Newbury); *The Rape of Lucretia* (Britten-Pears Festival, Snape Maltings Aldeburgh); *Hysteria* (Inspectors Sands, China/*Tsieina*); *Dolls* (National Theatre of Scotland, Glasgow).

Katharine was nominated for a 2008 Knight of Illumination Award for *I Am Falling* (Gate Theatre).
Derbyniodd Katharine enwebiad am Wobr Knight of Illumination 2008 ar gyfer I Am Falling (Gate Theatre).

Simon Allen
Music and Sound/
Cerddoriaeth a Sain

Simon creates work in all fields of music and sound. He is actively involved in free improvisation, contemporary music and has recently worked as a producer on *Under Ubi's Tree* by Nathan Thomson, released by the audiophile label Naim. Simon is creative director of Seeing in the Dark, a disability and human rights project in Bangladesh and India.
Mae Simon yn creu gwaith ym meysydd cerddoriaeth a sain. Mae e'n gweithio'n rheolaidd gyda phrosiectau byrfyfyr rhydd, cerddoriaeth gyfoes ac yn ddiweddar fel cynhyrchydd ar Under Ubi's Tree *gan Nathan Thomson, sydd wedi ei rhyddhau ar y label ansawdd uchel Naim. Simon yw cyfarwyddwr creadigol Seeing in the Dark, prosiect hawliau dynol ac anabledd ym Mangladesh ac India.*

Theatre/Theatr
Includes/*Yn cynnwys*: *Wunschkonzert/Request Programme* (Schauspiel Cologne); *Women Of Troy, Waves, Seagull, A Dream Play, The Tempest* (National Theatre); *Maes Terfyn* (Sherman Cymru); *Not The End Of The World, The Seagull* (Bristol Old Vic); *Measure For Measure, The Taming Of The Shrew* (Theatre Royal Plymouth/Thelma Holt); *The Blue Room* (Ustinov); *Buzz, Diwrnod Dwynwen* (Sgript Cymru); *The Nest, Andromache, Free From Sorrow, The Memory of Water* (Living Pictures Productions). As Co-arranger and Performer/*Fel Cyd-drefnydd a Pherfformiwr: Through Wood, The Tom Waits Project* (Opera North); projects with/prosiectau gyda: Young Vic, RSC, Shakespeare's Globe Theatre.

Film/Ffilm
Scores include/*Sgoriau yn cynnwys*: *Stalk, Tree, Sea Change* (Slinky Pictures).

Liz Ranken
Movement Director/
Cyfarwyddwr Symud

Liz is a director, choreographer, performer, writer and painter. She was a founder member of DV8 Physical Theatre and has been the recipient of the Time Out award for "Bringing Theatre Alive with Music". Liz has just written a multimedia play, *Starblast*.
Mae Liz yn gyfarwyddwr, coreograffydd, perfformiwr, awdur ac arlunydd. Roedd hi'n un o sylfaenwyr DV8 Physical Theatre ac mae hi wedi derbyn gwobr "Bringing Theatre Alive with Music" Time Out. Mae Liz newydd ysgrifennu ddrama amlgyfrwng, Starblast.

Theatre/Theatr
Includes/*Yn cynnwys*: *Summat-A-Do Wi' Weddings* (Palace Theatre - Place Portfolio Choreographic Award); *Funk Off Green* (Tramway Theatre - Edinburgh Fringe Capital Award); *Noughts and Crosses, The Henry Cycle, A Midsummer Night's Dream, Cymbeline, Winter's Tale, Pericles* (Royal Shakespeare Company); *Fire Face* (Royal Court); *Jane Eyre, The Mill on the Floss, Anna Karenina* (Shared Experience).

www.lizranken.com

Ben Tyreman
Stage Manager/
Rheolwr Llwyfan

Ben studied Drama at the University of Hull and completed a Postgraduate Diploma at the Webber Douglas Academy of Dramatic Art. He works as an actor, director, and freelance production/company/stage manager.
Astudiodd Ben Drama ym Mhrifysgol Hull a chyflawnodd Diploma Ôl-Raddedig yn y Webber Douglas Academy of Dramatic Art. Mae e'n gweithio fel actor, cyfarwyddwr a rheolwr cynhrychiad/cwmni/llwyfan ar ei liwt ei hun.

Theatre/Theatr
As an actor includes/*Fel actor yn cynnwys*: *The Dumb Waiter* (Sheffield Crucible). *Coriolanus* (Top of The World Theatre Company); *Amadeus*, *Skylight* (Gulbenkian Theatre); *Bad Girls* (Watershed/Polka Theatre); *Hamlet, Houdini & Sir Arthur* (Attic Theatre Company); *The Visit* (Edinburgh Fringe Festival); *You Can't Take it With You, The Good Doctor, Road, As You Like It* (Chanticleer Theatre); *Cinderella, Aladdin, Jack and the Beanstalk, Sleeping Beauty, Peter Pan* (Hiss & Boo Ltd.).

Other work includes/*Gwaith arall yn cynnwys*: *Kontakt, Small Change, 7 Sins, Judgement of Paris, The Pajama Men* (Assembly Rooms, Gilded Balloon, Edinburgh Festival); *Topless Mum* (Tobacco Factory/Tricycle Theatre, London); *The Caretaker* (Sheffield Crucible/Tricycle Theatre); *Handful of Henna, Long and the Short and the Tall, Topdog/Underdog* (Sheffield Crucible); *This Is So Not About The Simpsons* (Assembly Rooms, Edinburgh Festival).

Rachel Burgess
Deputy Stage Manager/Dirprwy Reolwr Llwyfan

Rachel studied Stage Management & Technical Theatre at the Royal Welsh College of Music and Drama.
Astudiodd Rachel Rheoli Llwyfan a Theatr Technegol yng Ngholeg Brenhinol Cerdd a Drama Cymru.

Theatre/Theatr
As Deputy Stage Manager includes:/*Fel Dirprwy Reolwr Llwyfan yn cynnwys*: *Maes Terfyn* (Sherman Cymru); *Kindertransport* (Aberystwyth Arts Centre Productions); *Cinderella* (Channel Theatre Productions); *Temptation* (Music Theatre Wales); *Atrium Opening Launch* (Mr Producer); *RWCMD Actors' Showcase '08 & '09.*

Other projects include/*Prosiectau eraill yn cynnwys*: *For You* (Music Theatre Wales); *Wales Rally GB Closing Ceremony* (CCC Events Team); *Eisteddfod Genedlaethol Live Television Shows* (Production 78).

Amgen : Broken

By/Gan **Gary Owen**

Characters/Cymeriadau:
Gary
Gareth

Dalier Sylw Publications
Cyhoeddiadau Dalier Sylw

Y Cinio (Geraint Lewis)
Hunllef yng Nghymru Fydd (Gareth Miles)
Epa yn y Parlwr Cefn (Siôn Eirian)
Wyneb yn Wyneb (Meic Povey)
"i" (Jim Cartwright – Welsh trans./*cyf. Cymraeg* John Owen)
Fel Anifail (Meic Povey)
Croeso Nôl (Tony Marchant – Welsh trans./*cyf. Cymraeg* John Owen)
Bonansa! (Meic Povey)
Tair (Meic Povey)

Sgript Cymru Publications
Cyhoeddiadau Sgript Cymru

Diwedd y Byd / Yr Hen Blant (Meic Povey)
Art and Guff (Catherine Treganna)
Crazy Gary's Mobile Disco (Gary Owen)
Ysbryd Beca (Geraint Lewis)
Franco's Bastard (Dic Edwards)
Dosbarth (Geraint Lewis)
past away (Tracy Harris)
Indian Country (Meic Povey)
Diwrnod Dwynwen (Fflur Dafydd, Angharad Devonald, Angharad Elen, Meleri Wyn James, Dafydd Llywelyn, Nia Wyn Roberts)
Ghost City (Gary Owen)
AMDANI! (Bethan Gwanas)
Community Writer 2001-2004 (Robert Evans, Michael Waters and others/*ac eraill*)
Drws Arall i'r Coed (Gwyneth Glyn, Eurgain Haf, Dyfrig Jones, Caryl Lewis, Manon Wyn)
Crossings (Clare Duffy)
Life of Ryan... and Ronnie (Meic Povey)
Cymru Fach (Wiliam Owen Roberts)
Orange (Alan Harris)
Hen Bobl Mewn Ceir (Meic Povey)
Aqua Nero (Meredydd Barker)
Buzz (Meredydd Barker)

Sherman Cymru Publications
Cyhoeddiadau Sherman Cymru

Maes Terfyn (Gwyneth Glyn)
The Almond and The Seahorse (Kaite O'Reilly)
Yr Argae (Conor McPherson – Welsh trans./Cyf. Cymraeg Wil Sam Jones)

Available from/*Ar gael o*:
Sherman Cymru, Senghennydd Rd, Cardiff, CF24 4YE.
Sherman Cymru, Ffordd Senghennydd, Caerdydd, CF24 4YE
029 2064 6901

ONE

There are two men on stage.
One, Gary, talks like this.
While the other, Gareth, talks like this.
They are both certainly aware of one another, and of the audience.

The one who talks like this, is finishing a packet of crisps as the show starts.

I want to tell you how a girl called Rachel saved my life.

A wi moyn gweud 'tho chi am sut 'naeth – rhywbeth arall achub 'mywyd i.
Wi'n rhy embarrassed i weud beth, yn gymwys.

For my life to be saved it must have needed saving.

Mae stori fi yn dechrau tamaid bach ar ôl stori fe. Na i jyst aros nes bod rhywbeth 'da fi i gyfrannu.

It could start with anything.
Say I make a plucky attempt to leave the house.
I open the front door, and there, on the pavement before me, I am confronted by

The Welsh-speaker drops his crisp packet.

A crisp packet.
Now it's important you understand that what bothers me is not so much the crisp packet itself.
It's more, the process by which it gets to be on the pavement.

Someone has been eating this packet of crisps and finished them, and this individual has – what?
Let his hand fall to his side? Let the grip of his fingers relax?
Let the greasy plastic flutter through the air.
And then he's just – walked on. Entirely careless.
What sort of person, what sort of mentality, lets that happen?

Rydw i –

I'll tell you what sort of mentality.

Rydw i –

The mentality of scum.

Rydw i – yn hoffi coffi.

Before I can take even one step onto the street this terrifying vision of a crisp packet I see before me confirms I am hemmed in on all sides by a scum mentality, which is creating a sea of shit and drowning human civilisation in it.
In the sea of shit which I aforementioned.

Rydw i yn hoffi coffi, gyda llaeth.
Rydw i'n hoffi coffi, gyda llaeth ac un . . . uh llwyed? o siwgr.
Ie: rydw i'n hoffi coffi, gyda llaeth, ac un llwyed o siwgr.

This is the state the world puts me in.

Fydde hi'n gweud, 'how do you say, "I like coffee" Gareth?', a 'swn i'n gweud, "Wi'n lico coffi," Miss.'

I'm using crisp packets as an example here, it's not just crisp packets that have this effect.

It's any sort of detritus left lying around by scum who don't give a toss whether we live or die.
People say sometimes I overreact to these things? I take them too seriously?
People sit me down and talk to me in soothing tones. They remind me that

Ac wedyn fydde hi'n gweud, 'Na. Na, Gareth. Nid, wi'n lico coffi.

That there is good in the world also, blah blah –

Rydw i yn hoffi coffi.' Ac 'swn i'n gweud,

and I should let the good balance the not-so-hot, blah blah,

'Wel, croeso i ti neud, beth bynnag ti MOYN i dy goffi di, Miss, –

Blah, blah-blah blah blah blah, blah blah-blah blah BLAH blah blah blah-blah blah, Blah, –

ond wi'n mynd i gario 'mlaen yn lico 'nghoffi i, diolch.'

And when these people speak to me

Obviously 'nes i ddim rîli gweud unrhywbeth fel 'na wrth fy athrawes.

obviously I try and listen.

'Nes i jyst – cadw'n dawel.

Yes, before next time I will make that list of three things I'm grateful for. This has been really helpful, I'm feeling so much more – like I have hope now, thank you, really thanks for your time.

Mae fe'n ffycd, obviously.

See – sometimes I think I can understand bits of what they're saying, but . . .

Yn yr hen dyddiau, 'sech chi'n marw, fydden nhw ddim yn gweud 'tha chi. Y syniad o'dd, i chi cael mwynhau eich diwrnodau olaf.

No. Getting nothing. You're wasting your breath.

Heddwch cyn i chi huno.

Even if I stay in, there's no escape. Some people – even though we live in terraced houses, and should be aware of our neighbours – some people play music or the television very loud indeed.
There is traffic and very regularly, there are sirens.
People walk up the road, carrying on drunken arguments.
And then you hear children walking past, and children –
Well children can be very cruel.
Children cannot wait for society to collapse.
The moment the police are no longer an effective force, it'll be gangs of tanned, skinny rat children roaming the place on their bikes, foraging in the ruins of supermarkets for crisps and alcopops.
There will be orgies of rape and torture, the first victims of which will be the fat kids and the weak kids.
Then with the fat and the weak all dead, the rat children will move on to you and I, my friends.
You, sir; and you, madam.
You are almost certainly dead meat.
Because you look like the kind of person who, ultimately, would not be able to stove in the head of ten year old child with a cricket bat.

The Welsh-speaker is considering another packet of crisps.

Pacedi . . . creision. Ti'n gweud 'pacedi creision', ac mae'n swnio i fi fel bo ti'n sôn am pacedi sy'n llawn creision. Yn hytrach na – y pacedi, y bagiau plastig eu hunain.
So os mae rhywun yn sôn i fi am bacedi creision ar y stryd, wi'n gweld actiwal pacedi llawn o greision, dros y palmant.
'Na i gyd wi'n meddwl yw – ai smokey bacon ydyn nhw? Achos dyna 'n hoff flas o greision. Er fydda i'n bwyta unrhyw flas o greision rîli.

People think sometimes I'm pessimistic.
But I'm not. Far from it.
I believe every new day is a chance to turn it all around.
I think we will have plenty of opportunities. Moments when an ordinary person, displaying extraordinary heroism, might just save us all.
So for example, madam, imagine the moment when the rat children are kicking at your door.
On that glorious day, your chance will have come.
Because instead of waiting to be dragged from your home and killed, you charge out, bellowing your righteous fury.
And you raise your cricket bat, and crush the skull of a piece of human scum.
And you go on swinging your cricket bat, until the sheer weight of their numbers tells against you and you go down, stoving in children's heads to the last.
And yes, you would die. But if everybody followed your example – if everyone here, now, committed to selling their lives dearly, taking three four or five rat children with them when they go – then surely we, the forces of civilisation, would win.

Wedi gweud hynny – salt and vinegar. Wi ddim rîli yn lico salt and vinegar.

To the English-speaker –

A ti ddim yn lico salt and vinegar chwaith?

But that won't happen.

Achos ti'n cael ulcers lot, ond wyt ti?

Instead you will let yourself be killed.

Ac mae'r vinegar'n rîli brifo dy ulcers di . . .

Because of some squeamishness – or let's call it what it is.
Cowardice.
And because of your cowardice, the rat children will never be stopped and it will be game over for the world as we know it.
It's the fact that the end of world could be averted, if only enough of us gave a shit – that's what tortures me.

So ie. Dyna be' sy'n dod i'n meddwl i, os mae rhywun yn sôn am bacedi creision – ydw i'n gallu bwyta nhw?

My essential optimism, is what makes it all so painful.

The English-speaker can go on no longer.

Yr athrawes 'na, o'dd yn obsessed gyda'r hoffi-ing the coffi – hi o'dd yr unig profiad annymunol neu anodd ges i gyda'r Gymraeg.
Allwn i fod wedi casáu'r iaith mewn ffordd. Pan 'naeth rhieni fi ysgaru, symudais i gyda mam pum milltir lan yr hewl i Glynderwen.
A es i i'r ysgol, troi lan ar y diwrnod cynta – i ffeindio bod pawb yn siarad iaith gwahanol i fi.
O'dd hyn yn bach o sioc. Achos cyn 'ny, o'n i ddim cweit wedi sylweddoli bod ieithoedd arall i gael yn y byd.
A gweud y gwir, sa i'n credu o'n i 'di syweddoli bod ieithoedd yn y byd.

O'dd e i gyd yn bach yn od.
Ond ti'n gwbod fel mae plant. Ymhen chwe mis o'dd fi a brawd fi yn brablan yn Gymraeg, a dim clem 'da mam beth o'n ni'n gweud. Pob tro fydde mam yn cwrdd â un o'n athrawon, fydde hi'n mynnu bod nhw ddim yn trafod yr un bachgen. Yn ôl fy athrawon, o'n i'n hapus, llawn egni, cyfeillgar. Ac yn ôl mam, o'n i mwy –

The Welsh-speaker looks at the English-speaker. The English-speaker reacts instantly.

What? What you staring at me for? Why don't you leave me alone? You don't understand me or my music!

Wi'n meddwl bod yr eglurhad yn rîli syml. O'dd yr ysgol yn un hyfryd. Wyth deg, naw deg ohonyn ni yno, pob athro yn nabod pob plentyn.
A 'nes i ffrindiau hyfryd yno. O'n i'n ffrindiau mawr 'da boi o'r enw Luke Osmond, o'dd ei dad, Osi, – nid yn baentiwr – o'dd e'n paentio lluniau yn yr ystyr neud celf, timod.
Gyda bechgyn fel arfer ma' 'na elfen o gystadleuaeth mewn bron pob cyfeillgarwch, yn arbennig pan ti'n ifancach.
Luke o'dd fy ffrind cyntaf o'dd yn mwy o gefnogwr, na rhywun i gystadlu gyda. O'dd e'n rîli golygus, a poblogaidd, ac o'dd y merched i gyd yn ffansïo fe –

To the English-speaker –

Ti'n cofio?
– eniwei.
Lwc, o'dd e.
Achos yn yr ysgol 'na, ac yn Gymraeg, o'dd hi fel ffeindio teulu fach saff a chynnes.
Adre o'n i jyst yn obsessed gyda'r rhyfel niwcliyr anochel o'dd yn mynd i ladd fi a mam, a brawd fi, a ci fi – a llysdad fi.

Yn anffodus, ar ôl dwy flynedd symudon ni o Glynderwen i Ben-y-Bont ar Ogwr.
Lle o'dd yr ysgol ddim mor fach. Lle o'dd y kids ddim cweit mor hyfryd, a diniwed.
A lle o'dd neb yn siarad Cymraeg – heblaw am y ferch 'na o'dd yn obsessed 'da'r coffi-hoffi-ing.

D'you think I'm just talking nonsense?
That civilisation can't collapse?

Ti ddim yn sylweddoli, pan ti'n ifanc – pa mor fregus ma' dy hapusrwydd.

Civilisations collapse all the time. They're such beautifully fragile things.

Os wyt ti'n hapus, wrth gwrs.

Say, Liberia. Civil war there. Saw a feature about it on News 24. They'd drag a family onto the streets and hold the husband, and he'd have to watch while the son was made to rape the mother and the sisters. Then they'd torture the men a bit, gang rape all the women, and leave the lot of them broken on the floor.
That's not rage, that's not a thing done in the heat of battle.
It's not lust even.
Someone's thought about that.
Someone has thought hard about how to destroy people, make them hate themselves and their loved ones.
Be kinder, once you've done stuff like that to people, just to kill the poor bastards.
Unless of course you believe in the limitless power of the human spirit to heal and forgive, in which case, it would be kinder to let them live.
More and more these days . . . I wonder whether I do believe,

in the limitless power of the human spirit.
I mean I say I do but . . . do I? Really?

Sa i moyn slago off Pen-y-Bont, ond –
– 'naeth y lle ddim gweithio i fi. Rhywsut – es i'n styc 'na.
Ac arhosais i'n styc 'na, nes i fi ddysgu Cymraeg 'to.
A dyna ni. Dyna'r stori sydd 'da fi i weud heddi.
Y stori sydd 'da fi i weud yw – wait for it – sut 'naeth dysgu'r iaith Gymraeg achub fy mywyd.
Wedais i bod e'n embarrassing.

Maybe you think, yeah okay, in Liberia or Yugoslavia or Germany sixty years ago but that nasty stuff, never here –
This is from some pissant satellite town, just outside London.
Two teenage girls were kidnapped by a gang of six young men.
The girls were taken to a hotel room. The young men told them they were going to be tortured, for hours, and then killed.
They boiled water in the crappy little hotel room kettle. Then tipped sugar, I'm guessing from the complimentary tea and coffee tray, into the boiling water, to make a kind of syrup.
Imagine having that thought. We could just pour boiling water onto their thighs but – even better, a syrup will be sticky, and will adhere to bare skin.
That way the pain will go on and on, for so much longer.
And imagine – taking the little packets of sugar from the tea and coffee tray.
Ripping the packets open, one by one, emptying them into the kettle.
Giving the mixture a stir. With the teaspoon provided.

Nid i ti ddigwyddodd hyn. So . . . yr holl ail-greu'r manylion bach arswydus, be' mae hynny'n actiwali . . .

Before they started, they put down towels on the carpet.

. . . ffyc beth yw'r gair?

To catch the mess.

Na. Wedi mynd. Os o'dd e yna yn y lle cyntaf.

Is that not enough? Okay, what about the kids who kicked a homeless woman to death and as she died pissed in her face and filmed it on their phones and looked into camera and said, 'This'll look great on YouTube'.

A nest ti edrych ar y ffilm? Ar YouTube? Betia i nest ti.

Or the man walking home from a night on the piss in Swansea who got knocked down on a dual carriageway and he was run over six times. By six different vehicles. And none of them stopped. Except one, where the driver got out to remove bloodied clothing from the bonnet of his car.

Achos ti'n gwynebu'r gwirionedd, ond wyt?

And if you want a nice, comforting moral at the end of those stories –
– well I've got one. Weren't expecting that, were you? But like I say, eternal optimist, thus the pain.
See one of the girls from the hotel torture orgy scenario survived.
When they shot her, the bullet bounced off her skull, ploughed across her scalp and exited her body leaving only superficial wounds.
She survived, testified, and those six murdering bastards are now all in prison.
So, yay! The system works.
Who knows, with the limitless power of the human spirit to heal and forgive, she may yet make for herself a life.

But of course the murdering bastards are all very young men.
Late teens, early twenties.
They'll be out in ten, fifteen years' time. And when they get out, they'll still be strong enough to, say, physically overpower any of our children.
I don't suppose any of you – any of the gentlemen perhaps? – fancy meeting me outside a prison in ten or fifteen years' time, and just killing them the second they walk free?
No, not the second. The second after.
Let them taste that first breath of freedom, and then –
Come on. We'd get away with it.
We would. Respectable people like us.

Mae hynny yn rhywbeth addawol iawn, wi'n credu.
Bod ti dal yn gweld dy hunan fel rhywun parchus.

The English-speaker smiles uncertainly at the Welsh-speaker. Gives him a big thumbs-up.

Er bod ti ar y dole ac yn methu gadael y tŷ ac yn treulio bron pob dydd yn y gwely yn cuddio o'r byd tu fas.

Actually, in spite of my problems, I do manage to leave the house on occasion.
Because alternate Thursdays I have to sign on.
I know what you're thinking – oh how convenient, the day there's money on the line, suddenly he has the strength to drag himself out of bed.
But that's a very negative way of looking at things.
Another way of looking at the situation is to say that I use the necessity of going out and signing on, as a sort of lever.
A means of getting myself out of bed and into the world.
Because I do appreciate that's what needs to happen. Getting out there. Interacting. Simple things like going for a walk.
You're sort of – walking to recovery?

And if you can look at things in a more positive way, then – why not?

Pan ddechreuais i ddysgu Cymraeg, des i i ddibynnu eitha lot ar y geirau, 'Pam lai?'. Pan ti'n ymarfer sgwrsio, fyddi di er enghraifft yn esgus neud rhyw blan i fynd i rhywle ar wyliau. So fydd dy bartner yn gweud 'Liciet ti bo ni'n mynd am dro, i ni gael mwynhau awyr twym y cyfnos, a sŵn hyfryd plant yn chwarae ar y strydoedd?'
A ti'n gweud – 'Pam lai?'.

Pam? Lie?

Ie, pam lai?

I'm sorry I don't know anyone of that name.

Mae'n amazingly handy, achos – os ti'n jyst gweud, 'Ie,' neu, yn fwy gywir, 'Liciwn', ti 'di rhoi stop ar y sgwrs –

Handy!

– ac mae'n amlwg bod bygar-ôl 'da ti i weud.

Bugger all!

Ond os ti'n gweud yn gyflym 'Pam lai?', ti'n edrych yn rîli rhugl a cyfforddus yn yr iaith, ac hefyd ti'n pasio'r pêl nôl i dy bartner. Ac mae dy bartner yn gorfod meddwl am rhywbeth go sylweddol i weud.

Go go go! Going for gold!

Felly – tro nesa ti'n styc am rhywbeth i weud, pam lai treial 'pam lai'?

Nope. No. Losing me there.

Neu, ti'n colli dy hunan.

So alternate Thursdays it was almost as a kind of therapy that I would leave the house to sign on.

Wi'n gwbod bod ti'n deall fi.

Often though it would take me a while to get up.

Rhaid bo' ti yn.

Then a while longer forcing myself to unlock the front door.

Os wi'n deall y geiriau 'ma, rhaid bod ti yn hefyd.

So by the time I got into town, it would be two in the afternoon. Two getting on for three.

Ond ti'n gwrthod deall.

Three o'clock in the afternoon is of course a danger time. Because that's when the rat children start spilling out of school. And the day tips towards twilight.

Na, na: mae hynny'n rong.

If it got to three o'clock, I would have to take refuge.

Ti yn deall, ti'n methu stopio deall.

And cafés make me nervous.

Ti'n gwrthod cydnabod bo ti'n deall.

The way people bump the back of your chair, as they're trying to get past?

Ti'n dewis bod fel wyt ti.

So I'd get a paper, slip into a pub.

A – pam lai?

The Roof, was a favourite.
Not a favourite in the sense that I liked it.
But in the sense that it was where I tended to go, at about three in the afternoon, on alternate Thursdays.
There would always be a few boys there, people I knew who they were because we'd been in school together for about eleven years; but not people I would ever have spoken to. Don't know why, exactly, just didn't move in the same circles –

O'n i ddim yn siarad â nhw, achos o'n i'n ffycin casáu nhw.

But it's like if you're away somewhere, and you see a face you recognise from home and you find yourself stopping and saying hello, even if you don't really know them?
It was a bit like that. We were three or four young men, we knew each others' faces from school.
We knew that if we were better people, we'd have something better to do on a Thursday afternoon than sit nursing pints in the Roof.
So we'd sit and nurse together.
It was an awkward gathering, at times.
We didn't have much in common.

Heblaw am chwant peint yn y prynhawn.

The English-speaker looks at the Welsh-speaker.

Rhywbeth sy'n uno ni i gyd, siwr o fod.

I tried to take it as a sign of my growing maturity, that I was able to share a pint with people I'd once hated.
Except of course what I was really doing was getting myself drunk enough that I could face the walk home even though there might be rat children in the underpass or on the black path or at any of the nineteen bus stops or three convenience shops I would pass on my way.
And it's one such Thursday that Rachel comes into the pub. And she is the one who saves my life. All this up till now has been just by way of making clear to you that I was actually in trouble and my life did need saving.
Is that clear?

Ie.

Do you need a bit more detail –

Na.

– on how fucked-up I was?

Na.

Because I can go on.

Plîs, na.

There are many more horrible things in my head I could share

NA, NA, ER MWYN IESU NA!

Is that a no?

Ie.

Is that a yes?

The Welsh-speaker nods.

Shall I just get to the my life being saved by a girl called
Rachel bit?

Pam lai?

Again, it's Rachel, not Pam: and Rachel was a girl who had
always annoyed me.
One thing you noticed about her was, she was sexy.
People can be pretty, or beautiful: but you can be both those
things, without being sexy.
Rachel was pretty, and on occasion beautiful as well: but more
than either of those, she was sexy.
Like I say it really got on my tits.
I've wondered a lot about what exactly it is, that makes someone
sexy.
And I think it's something really simple.

Mae nhw'n neud ti moyn ffycio nhw.

The English-speaker looks at the Welsh-speaker.

Os mae rhywun yn neud ti moyn ffycio nhw, mae nhw'n secsi.

I'm not sure I like your tone there.
No, a girl is sexy when she knows you want to do things to her;
and she doesn't mind.
I'm not saying she's going to let you do things to her, or she gets
off on you wanting to do things to her.
But she knows that you have these feelings about her – and

she lets you have them.
She doesn't comment on them. Say, in her body language.
She doesn't project disgust.
And so you find yourself being quite comfortable about, you know: all your desperate tearful lust, when you're in her presence.
That's what Rachel did.
She materialised in the doorway, looked round for someone she knew – 'cause of course she'd know someone – then came right over, plonked herself down. Unasked, uninvited – un-bloody-believable.
She sat there at our table, chatting happily away.
Each of us wanting to tear her clothes off and fuck her raw.
Her knowing, and completely comfortable with it.
Utterly unflapped by our raging desire.
Amazing, the arrogance of the woman.
I wasn't going to put up with that, so I wandered off.
See I had this thing, at the time – where I was doing really well with girls?
It sounds ridiculous, I was this mess who could barely leave the house but when I did get out and into the pub, I pulled, almost every fortnight.
I think it was that I was so fucking desperate.
People say desperation isn't attractive.
But you work with what you've got.
My desperation would sweep across the pub like a radar beam and every now and again I'd get an answering 'ping'.
Contact, three o'clock high.
Some still pert young wife in the corner. With the nagging feeling that marriage and motherhood haven't been – quite the adventure she'd hoped for.
Along I come, a buzzy little drunk insisting that she is the one who is going to save my life.
Ninety minutes later I'm going down on her and she's wondering aloud how risking her husband, her family and

everything that matters could possibly feel so . . . innocent.
I say to her –

Paid.

– that innocence,

Paid.

it's a gift we're giving one another.

Jesus.

No I really do. I say things like that, and I get away with it.

The English-speaker stops.

I wish I hadn't told you that now.

Be' wedais i?

Because that, again, that was a true thing.
The girl who spoke those words to me, I wasn't just using her.
I mean obviously I was.
But if things had been different.
If she hadn't've met her husband before she met me, I swear to God – I would've crossed continents for her.
Always assuming I was able to leave the house.

Wi'n credu ti, brawd.

You credit me? Really?

Colled hi, 'naeth hi setlo 'da boi arall. Dylai hi 'di aros amdanat ti.

And . . . we're losing signal again.

The English-speaker gets back to telling his story.

So I'm trying what moves I've got on every girl in the pub whose outfit speaks more of hope than confidence and getting nowhere.
I'm thinking I've probably taken a maximum dose of rejection for one evening and I can't really be hurt any more so I slide up to Rachel at the bar and I say to her, only losers come back to this shithole town, what the fuck's gone wrong with you?
She says – it's Gary, right?
I say yes, it's Gary, that's a hundred per cent correctamundo.
She goes you're probably going to feel really horrible about having said that.
I go I feel really fucking horrible most of the fucking time so you just trowel it on, sister.

Chwarae teg – o't ti'n horrendously pissed ar y pryd.

I was pissed, obviously.
Rachel looks at me a bit and says, my mum's got cancer.
Just drops that bomb. No preamble.
They haven't caught it early, apparently, and things are not looking good.
And this afternoon, they'd admitted her mum to a hospice.
Rachel had stayed around for the settling in, hopped on a bus back into town, and walked in the first pub she saw.
Obviously there's an opening at this point for me to stop all my bullshit and just tell her how sorry I am?
But if I do that, suddenly coming over all apologetic, it's going to look fake as hell.
Rachel's waiting for me to react but I've made my decision and I'm sticking to it.

And after a bit Rachel does something a bit weird like she sneezes or gasps at me; and then she smiles.
A frosty smile, if I'm honest.
She pays for the round, plonks a pint of Fosters in front of me and says, you enjoy your beer.
Spills quite a lot of the pint, actually, as she puts it down.
Makes a fair bit of mess.
Rachel goes back to the table and after a while 'cause I don't know what else to do, I do as well.
Everyone else is blabbering on about nothing.
And at some point Rachel stops blabbering on.
Then after a bit she sort of – slumps towards me and starts talking about – her mum and how difficult it is and she's so tired, she catches herself hoping for it to end and then realising what she's hoping for is her mum's death, and what kind of a woman does that make her?
And she uses that word, 'woman', about herself and it seems a bit unnecessary. A bit I suppose explicit.
And that gets me annoyed with her again.
Then they call chucking out and turn the lights on, and Rachel blinks a bit.
It seems she's been crying but I hadn't noticed.
She leans in close, says, look thanks for letting me offload all this on you.
I can feel her breath on my ear and everything so obviously that gets me fucking furious.
I say, we both know you think I'm a tosser, so what the fuck are you doing still talking to me, eh?

Cwestiwn wi 'di ofyn i'n hunan, weithiau.

The next thing was, me and Rachel are outside the pub having a sort of fight.
Not physical, just shouting.

One of the bouncers goes, look love either punch his lights out or fuck him I don't care which but could you move it on please? So we head back to mine for a few more drinks and both have a bit of a sob.
I'm not sure what I'm crying about.
Just joining in, I think.
And then she leans on my shoulder.
And then we're cuddling.
And then kissing.
And then fucking.
And I'm not gonna lie to you, it is

He considers for a bit.
And then stops considering.

See I would say it is an epiphanous moment, but half of you won't know what that means and the other half'll think it's just a horrible cliché.
But sod you, it was a truly great moment for me.
To be finally fucking Rachel Jones, having fantasised about it for most of my school career.
And I make sure I stuck it in her mouth, while I've got the chance.
Because I mean, I'm fairly certain this encounter is going to be a one-off.
You see, I take for granted Rachel is sleeping with me 'cause she's in a vulnerable emotional state, rather than because she genuinely likes me.
That's how low my self-esteem has sunk.

Ie, 'sgwn i pam?

See that's not –
– that's not sounding very supportive.

Wi'n treial fod yn gefnogol ond Christ so ti'n neud hynny yn hawdd.

Christ, you actually hate me, don't you.

Sa i'n casáu ti.

Yeah, course you do.

Wi'n teimlo piti drosto ti.

And in fact I don't blame you.

The English-speaker returns to his story.

Rachel's mum died a few weeks later.
All her friends had moved away so, I was the closest thing Rachel had. To a friend.
I didn't really know what to say, by way of comfort or anything like that.
So I kept my mouth shut.
As it went, keeping it zipped was just what Rachel needed.
By saying nothing I gave her chance to pour it all out and when she was finished talking she'd have a bit of a cry.
Then we'd end up in bed.
It was a really happy time for me.
That sounds horrible, because obviously it was a really shitty time for her but – it's true.
I was basically living with Rachel, at her dead mum's house.
I was out of my mum's place, which was a relief.
Mornings Rachel would give me her cash card, I'd sortie out to Greggs, and load up with effortless eating – pasties, sandwiches, Welsh cakes. They did these gorgeous cheese and brocolli lattices back then that we both loved.

I'd wander home, stack the food in the fridge, disrobe once again, and head back to bed with Rachel.
We'd spend most of the day snoozing, watching TV, and having lazy sex.
But I don't think it was the sex, or the laziness, or the suddenly being able to leave the house that made that time so happy for me.
I think it was because for those weeks, being with Rachel while she grieved, I served a purpose.
Which I probably never had done before.

Ti ddim yn meddwl bod 'na wers i ti 'na?

Do it again?

Ti'n cadw dy geg ar gau am unwaith – ac mae pethau da'n digwydd.

Well that's easy for you to say.

Neu ti jyst yn sick fuck sy'n hapusach ymlith trasiedi.

The English-speaker turns back to the audience.

And that was the start. Because then, over the next few weeks, Rachel worked a sort of miracle.
You think miracle and you think something like – moving a mountain.
By your faith ye shall move mountains, the book says, and mentally you are visualising a mountain detaching from the landscape, lifting up into the sky and floating along to wherever you want it.
And if that ever happened, clearly, it would be a miracle.
Who would argue with that?
But another way to move a mountain would be to get a

shovel, go to the foot of a mountain, dig up a shovel-full of earth, then walk to where you want the mountain to be, and plonk your shovel-full of earth down.
If you did that enough times – millions of times probably – then you would move a mountain.
And if you actually spent years of your life moving a mountain, one shovel-full at a time, and you kept on till the whole damn mountain was moved – I say that would be a miracle as well.
Nothing supernatural involved but a miracle nonetheless.
It was that second kind of miracle Rachel did – on me. Or to me, or whatever.
A miracle of patience, and persistence, and determination.

Mae pethau bendigedig yn gallu digwydd. Hyd yn oed yng nghanol tristwch.

And maybe seeing a miracle in the middle of grief and loss and sadness – maybe that's just sick.

To the Welsh-speaker.

What d'you reckon?

He doesn't answer.

Rachel'd been studying medicine, to be a doctor.
Of course I was worried that at some point she'd head back to college.
But by the time she was recovered enough, it was too late to just pick up where she'd left off.
They said she'd have to wait, start afresh the following year.
In the Echo I noticed a firm of solicitors in town, looking for an office junior.
They were a bit suspicious at first, thought Rachel was over-

qualified but she lied, told them she was planning on going into law and then it all made sense.
I was safe, until at least September and the new year at college.
Or that's what I thought, but – with Rachel going to this new job, seeming like she was on the mend
That was hard for me.
When someone's grieving their dead mum and there's no food in the house, it's a bit embarrassing trying to explain you can't go down the shops 'cause of a crisp packet on the pavement.

Mae'n mwy na embarrassing. Mae'n amhosibl. Ti'n methu egluro 'ny. Ac felly ti'n gorfod jyst mynd i'r blydi siops, ond wyt?

But once that person is no longer so obviously grieving.
Once she's up and about, doing very well for herself in a new job – then things become a little bit more complicated.
Because what you know is, that she could just pop into the shops herself. On her way home from work, say.
There's no need for you to face the crisp packet on the pavement.
And sometimes it's good to be gentle with yourself.
So to begin with I had a bug. And I couldn't leave the house for fear of shitting myself in public.
Then the bug mutated into a migraine, brought on by eating too much chocolate, 'cause chocolate was all there was in the house, what with me being too ill to go to the shops.
After the migraine had lasted three days Rachel said perhaps we should call out the doctor.
I said like a doctor's gonna help, it'll just be more pills papering over the symptoms and never getting to the heart of the problem.
And Rachel said
Rachel said well fair enough I do see / your point

The Welsh-speaker interrupts

/ Rachel said, do you know what kind –

Don't you dare! Don't you bloody dare.

Stand-off.

Rachel said well / fair enough

/ Do you know what kind of person / has a splitting

/ No no no no no. You do not – no.

They stare at each other.

Do you know what kind / of person –

/ No no no that is mine.

Beat.

What kind of person has a splitting migraine headache for three days and then doesn't want to see a doctor who could prescribe them major painkillers and relieve their agony?

Oh that's low.

I said, like a doctor's gonna help, and Rachel said, what kind of person has a splitting migraine headache for three days and then doesn't want to see a doctor who could prescribe them major painkillers and relieve their agony?

I said no, I don't know, what kind of person is like that?
Rachel said, a person –

A person who doesn't have a migraine at all.

I'll do it, alright, I'll say it.
Rachel said,

a person who is faking it.

Yeah well this all led into quite an extended conversation, the details of which I don't need to repeat now, mainly 'cause it was about crisp packets and rat children and the collapse of civilisation, and I've told you lot that crap already.
When I'd told it all to Rachel there was a bit of a silence.
And then she said

Perhaps all that's happened is, you've been on the dole a while, you've got used to staying in, and now leaving the house seems like this massive thing.
When really it isn't.

I said that though my fears about crisp packets and rat children and the decline of civilisation were obviously to an extent exaggerated, they were nonetheless based in facts about today's society, and I wasn't prepared to bury my head in the sand and pretend those facts didn't exist.

Rachel said,

Right, you're refusing to bury your head in the sand – by refusing to leave the house?

And she laughed.
Obviously that upset me a bit.
She said,

And what about the fact that you can leave the house, if you really have to? Like to go and sign on? Or when there's no food in?

And then I said I didn't think it would help making me feel so attacked. Given that I felt attacked all the bloody time, even by litter on the streets.
Rachel said,

Well why don't you go and pick the litter up, if it bothers you so much?

I said well I would, if I could leave the house.
She said,

But of course you can't.

I said of course I can't, no.
She said,

And so – society collapses. 'Cause no-one picks the litter off the streets. Not even you, the person who spends his whole life worrying about it.

I said right let's cut the shit shall we? Now you know what a fucking loser I am, I'm dumped.
Aren't I?

Ni yn dod yn agos at y pwynt pan fydd rhyw fath o wahanu.

And Rachel came over, and leaned down, and kissed me.
Then she dropped to her knees, and took me in her mouth.
It is hard for any man to feel too bad about himself, while a beautiful and intelligent woman is hungrily sucking him off.
And I think Rachel knew that.
Afterwards we had a bit less of a doomy discussion about stuff.
Rachel said we had a good thing going between us, and she wanted it to carry on.
Of course I agreed with her on that one.

Rachel said, she didn't expect me to change.
I could just sit in the house, on the dole, for the rest of my life if I wanted to.
She wouldn't dump me, she wouldn't get annoyed with me or anything like that.
She'd just have one life out in the world; and another life home, with me.
There was no pressure.
I could stay as I was, if I wanted.
Just stop in the house, and each night, Rachel would come home to me.
I'd be in the house, Rachel'd be in the office.

Yn neud ffrindiau newydd.

I'd want her to make friends.

Cael hwyl gyda'r merched. A'r dynion.

And flirting in the workplace is fun and harmless.

Ond wedyn ti'n gweld pâr yn fflirtio dim ond gyda'i gilydd . . .

What could another bloke have that I haven't got?

Ffaith bod e'n gallu gadael y tŷ?

So you see: Rachel had trapped me.
Even staying in the house I had no shelter.
She had her plans, all worked out. Cause I'd been on the dole a while, there were all these courses I could go on? The first thing we did, was sign me up for one of those. It was basic computer skills, stuff I already knew – but that wasn't the point.

Anghofiast ti am y shiatsu.

Whassat?

Y shiat-su.

Oh yeah, actually – before all that, Rachel got a friend of hers round, who was practising to become a shiatsu therapist, and she gave me these shiatsu sessions.

A naethon nhw rîli helpu.

And I mean it's all bollocks, all this pre-modern nonsense about meridians and energy flows and that crap. I felt embarrassed going along with it. But you know what it's like – anything to keep the missus happy.

Falle jyst effaith cael rhywun yn gofalu amdana i, am awr dwy waith yr wythnos, wi ddim yn gwbod. Ond ar ôl cael y shiatsu, o'n i'n mwy – o'dd 'n meddwl i yn dawelach.

The first morning I was supposed to go to this computer class, I was shitting myself.
I was sat there on the floor in the hall, knowing I wasn't going to be able to move.
Then Rachel came downstairs in her coat and said, we off then? She opened the door, turned round, and held out her hand to me.
We chattered like idiots on the way, a bit forced like but keeping my mind off things nicely.
We got to the community centre and I turned to Rachel to say goodbye. She said – what d'you mean goodbye? I'm coming in too.
The bloke in charge couldn't find her name on any of the lists but Rachel smiled and said there must've been some mistake,

and the bloke melted and said yes of course there must've been.
He ticked my name off without looking at me. 'Cause he was still looking at Rachel.
The others were a mix of older blokes who didn't have a clue and were properly there to learn something – and then there were younger lads, wasters really, just there to get the dole off their backs.
I suppose I might've looked very much like one of them, to an outside eye.
They flocked round Rachel, the youngest to the oldest, all these wasters, all these human scum, thinking they were in with a chance.
And even though we'd come in together, none of them imagining that Rachel might be with me.
Because they looked at her, and they saw this gorgeous young woman, they looked at me, and they saw –

Be?

I didn't even show up on the scanner.
I spent that whole two hours thinking brilliant move Rach this is really helping the self-esteem.
Then, at the end of the class, Rachel called to me, across the room.
She said, Gary, isn't it? Would you fancy taking me for a drink?
And in a tone of voice implying this drink could be just the start of the things, if I played my cards even half-right.

Wi'n cofio'r eiliad 'na weithiau.

I loved her so much then.

A, cofio'r eiliad 'na, mae'n anodd credu beth wnes i iddi hi.

Next morning middle-aged hasbeens and young wasters alike crowded round me. I played very much the gentleman, wouldn't give any details whatsoever – I just discreetly intimated she was gagging for it but I hadn't done the deed 'cause I was being a smooth bastard and keeping her waiting till she was literally ready to beg.

Ond wedyn wi'n cofio – popeth – a wi'n ffeindio bo fi'n gallu maddeu 'n hunan.
Rhaid maddeu dy hunan yn y diwedd, ond oes?

Rachel said the next step was for me to deal with my fears about global environmental catastrophe.
I said I'd be very happy, if it were possible for me to do anything at all, to avert global environmental catastrophe, though I didn't think that was very bloody likely. Rachel produced a leafet about a group of conservation volunteers in town. They went out every Sunday, doing things like building footpaths and fences – plus picking up a lot of crisp packets and shit that the everyday scum leave behind.
I joined them.

'Naeth y gwaith 'na byd o les i fi. Jyst fod tu fas i'r dre, mas yn y cefn gwlad, bach o awyr ffres. A jyst neud rhywbeth hollol wahanol i unrhywbeth o'n i wedi neud o'r blaen. A cwrdd â phobl gwahanol. Pobl rîli hyfryd: pobl o'dd yn becso am y byd, fel fi, ond pobl o'dd yn benderfynol o neud rhywbeth i helpu, nid fel –

He stops himself.

O'n i'n mynd i weud 'nid fel fi'. Ond yn amlwg, 'nes i ddim ond cwrdd â'r pobl 'ma trwy fod mas yn treial neud rhywbeth i helpu. So actiwali –
– o'n nhw'n pobl o'dd yn becso am y byd, fel fi. Ac o'n nhw'n pobl o'dd yn benderfynol o neud rhywbeth i helpu. Fel fi.

Obviously what we were doing was very small-scale and you had to wonder how much it was really contributing to the wider project of saving the world from eco-catastrophe.
Say quite often we'd go down to Southerndown, or Ogmore by Sea, or Rest Bay, and we'd pick up shit off the beach. After we'd picked up all the shit, the beach would look great. We'd take pictures.
The beach before, draped in shit. The beach after, shit-free. And us, with a pile of sixty bin bags.

Diwrnod da o waith. A fydden ni 'di cael diwrnod da yn neud y waith, hefyd –

– most of these black bags would be full of plastics.
These plastics would never biodegrade, obviously, 'cause there's nothing in nature that eats plastics.

Yn yn fan ar y ffordd adre, 'swn i'n breuddwydio am Barafundle Bay, yn Sir Benfro, a jyst meddwl pa mor hyfryd fydde hi i fyw yn yr ardal 'na, a cael mynd am dro ar draeth Barafundle bob dydd. Ac wedyn 'swn i'n breuddwydio, tasai'r byd i gallio rhyw ddydd, a stopio rhoi shit yn y môr, wel yn y diwedd, fydde popeth o'dd wedi cael ei dympio yn y moroedd yn barod, ffeindio ei ffordd i Sir Benfro, a golchi lan ar Barafundle.
Felly, alli di glanhau moroedd y byd i gyd, jyst trwy mynd am dro ar draeth Barafundle pob dydd, a pigo lan beth bynnag 'nest ti ffeindio 'na.

And these people doing the conservation work: they were all of a type.
Lovely people, sure. Very concerned. But if they could've been doing anything that was really going to make a difference, would they've been getting their hands dirty picking up shit in Rest Bay?

No. They'd've been giving orders. Passing laws. Re-allocating budgets.
But none of them were people with that sort of clout.
They were the worried and powerless. Just like me.
Fighting off the fears that come in the night, with the thought that they had sacrificed six hours on a Sunday.
Again, just like me.
And what if six hours shit-picking a week isn't enough to save the world from eco-catastrophe?

Weithiau fydden ni'n cael mynd bant i rhywle, i neud prosiect dros penwythnos hir. Aethon ni lan unwaith i Sir Fôn, i neud dry-stone walling ar rhyw fferm tu fas i Amlwch.

You're saying about dry-stonewalling now.

Ie.

Tell them it was in Anglesey, 'cause that's really important.

Wi wedi neud.

As if the audience haven't been told this already –

This was in Anglesey this bit happened.

Glawiodd hi trwy'r tri diwrnod fuon ni'n gweithio, gwynt yn mynd syth trwydden ni. Aros mewn neuadd y pentre, yn cysgu ar y llawr, coginio ar camping stove. Dim cawod, dim dŵr poeth, dim teledu. Amser bendigedig. Na i fyth anghofio.
Y penwythnos 'na o'dd y tro cyntaf i fi, fel oedolyn, clywed y Gymraeg yn cael ei siarad fel iaith naturiol.
Wi'n cofio gwrando ar sgwrs y ffermwr a'r hen ddyn o'dd yn dangos i ni sut i neud y dry-stone walling, ac fod yn siocd pa mor estron o'dd yr iaith yn swnio.

Obviously Cymraeg Sir Fôn o'dd hyn, so . . . dim syndod mewn ffordd ond o hyd, o'dd rhyw lais fach tu fewn yn gweud, ar un adeg, Gareth, o't ti'n gallu deall yr iaith 'na.
Ar ddiwedd y penwythnos, daeth y ffermwr rownd gyda amlen bach i bob un ohonyn i. Tu fewn i'n amlen i, ffeindais i bapur pum punt.
O'dd y ffermwr 'di cael y gwaith 'di neud yn rhad wrth gwrs, gan taw volunteers o'n ni i gyd. Wedodd e, "thanciw feri mytsh boi bach, ffor helpyn mi whith mai wôls."

His accent – it was like he was speaking Welsh, even when he was speaking English? Cracked me up.

Wi'n cofio syllu ar y pum punt 'na yn meddwl, dyma pum punt wi 'di gweithio i gael, ac wedi mwynhau gweithio i gael, er bod y gwaith 'na wedi bod tu fas yn y glaw a'r gwynt.
Gyda'r pum punt, es i â Rachel mas i'r pyb lleol, a prynu drinc iddi hi.
Gyda arian o'n i wedi ennill 'n hun.

Of course technically I should've declared that five pounds to social security and they would've deducted it from my job-seeker's allowance.
So while I was sitting there congratulating myself on being a real man and earning my pay by the sweat of my brow, and triumphantly taking my woman out for a celebratory vodka and tonic – actually it was bollocks. I wasn't buying her a drink – the government was.

Actiwali, ti'n cael cadw y pum punt cyntaf ti'n ennill trwy neud gwaith rhan-amser tra bod ti ar y dôl. So fuck off.

Although it wasn't strictly a vodka and tonic.

Be' ti'n meddwl?

She asked for vodka and tonic, you were gonna have a Carlsberg.
But that would have cost five pound sixty. And in my hand, that precious fiver.

O'n i 'di anghofio 'ny.

Tonic is expensive. Ninety pee for one of those little bottles. She got her vodka, but with a splash of lemonade from the tap.

Wedodd hi dim byd. Yfodd hi'r drinc a gathon ni noswaith hyfryd. Mwy na thebyg 'naeth hi ddim hyd yn oed sylwi.

The English-speaker looks at him.

Ocê, 'naeth hi sylwi. Wrth gwrs o'dd hi'n gwbod y gwahanieth rhwng tonic a lemonade. Ond wedodd hi ddim byd.
Achos o'dd hi'n caru fi.

A moment.

Soon after that the computer course came to an end.
Rachel suggested I take on something new and I don't really know why, but I decided on Welsh.

'Nes i benderfynu ar Gymraeg oherwydd y profiad o glywed yr iaith yn cael ei siarad yn naturiol yn y Gogledd. Nawr o'n i'n gweld y Gymraeg nid jyst fel rhyw bwnc sych, academaidd, ond fel iaith bywiog a perthnasol i'r byd cyfoes. A hefyd o'dd y Gymraeg yn atgoffa fi o amser hapusach yn 'y mywyd.

Probably it was just that there's Welsh classes all over the place, they're so desperate for you to learn it.
I had time on my hands so I started on this quite intensive course. Two hours, three mornings a week.

It was good. Boring as fuck, especially to start with but – good to be out of the bed in the morning.
At the same time the company Rachel was working for made her an offer.
They said if she wanted to go into law they'd take her on permanently. They would train her on the job and release her part-time and in the end she'd be a solicitor.
Now Rachel was supposed to go back to college. She'd told them she wanted to be a solicitor, but only so they'd give her a job.
But say she did go back to college, what would that mean for me?
Where would I live?
Who would I live with?
Who would care for me?
She asked me my advice, and I didn't know what to tell her.

Cyfleus.

And in fact, who the hell was I, to be telling her what to do?

Ei chariad.

Obviously in some ways it wasn't an equal partnership. I'm not afraid of saying that.

O'dd y gwersi Cymraeg hefyd yn helpu fi creu rhyw fath o fywyd i fi fy hunan, a'r wahân i fod gyda Rachel.
Fydde'r tiwtoriaid yn trefnu trips a nosweithiau mas, i rhoi cyfle i ni ymarfer 'mewn cydestun anffurfiol'.
Y theori o'dd, fydden ni'n llai embarrassed am ddefnyddio ein crap Cymraeg os o'n ni i gyd yn feddw gaib.
O'dd y theori yn gweithio. Pan ti mor feddw ti'n gorfod canol-bwyntio'n eitha galed jyst er mwyn aros ar dy draed, yn aml iawn bydd dy ofn cam-dreiglo yn diflannu.

Things were getting more equal. I was more or less able to leave the house at will, I had my new computer skills, I had my shit-picking on a Sunday, I had my Welsh lessons, I had my new Welsh friends – I was doing great.

'Nes i rîli fwynhau y gwersi Cymraeg, mae'n rhaid i fi weud. Nid oherwydd y gwersi eu hunain – ond oherwydd y pobol 'nes i gwrdd. Andy Welsh – câth e'r enw achos, er bod e'n dod o Lundain, o'dd e wastad rîli mewn i bethau Cymreig. Rod, the Gay Canadian with the Massive . . . Harp. Pamela, yr awdures o Rhode Island – yr awdur go iawn cyntaf cwrddais i erioed. O'n i mor impressed 'da hi achos, ble bynnag o'n ni'n yfed, fydde hi wastad yn cael bourbon mawr, gyda un ciwb o iâ. Marion, y flonden o Berlin, o'dd yn gymaint o gomiwnist, pallodd hi ymuno â'r blaid, achos o'n nhw wedi bradychu ysbryd Marx. Ac wedyn Andrew and Mary, y ficars priod.

I was doing so great that sometimes I would joke that I was finished – as a project? And Rachel could move on, with a clear conscience.
She'd give me a bit of a look when I said things like that.

Ond o'dd hi jyst yn treial neud pethau'n well i ti.

And of course she wasn't going to abandon me. She couldn't.

Achos o'dd hi'n caru ti.

Because I still didn't have a job, and I was depending on her to keep me in the style I'd become accustomed to.
When she wanted me to get out there and start paying my own way – that's when I'd have to worry.
Or so I would say to her.
As a joke.
And she would give me

That bit of a look.

Achos o'dd hi'n caru ti.

I did dare to think sometimes
She was never going to abandon me, because she loved me.
But that became hard to believe

Ie. Wel.

In time.

O'dd hi'n caru ti, fel o'dd hi'n gallu.

A moment.

I've forgotten where I am.

Achos bod 'na rhywbeth ti 'di anghofio.

Whassat?

Neu wedi gadael mas, yn fwriadol.

Seriously, where am I?

Pan aethon ni ar y nosweithiau meddw, fydde un o ein tiwtoriaid wastad yno. Enw hi o'dd Lowri.
O'dd Lowri'n becso fi, rhaid gweud.
'Nes i ffeindio 'n hunan – o'n i jyst yn ymwybodol iawn ohoni hi.
O'n i'n ymwybodol iawn o'n i'n aros iddi hi gyrhaedd.
Wedyn o'n i'n ymbwybodol iawn pwy o'dd hi'n siarad gyda.
Beth o'dd hi'n gwisgo.
Faint o siâp ei chorff o'n i'n gallu gweld.

Mewn ffordd, o'dd y peth yn ddigon naturiol. O'dd fi a Rachel wedi bod 'da'n gilydd am sbel erbyn hyn, yn amlwg o'n i'n mynd i sylwi tasai ferch arall yn dechrau talu sylw ata i.
Ond o hyd o'n i dal yn teimlo bach yn ansicr am y peth.
So 'nes i sôn i Rachel am Lowri.
Obviously 'nes i ddim gweud, mae 'na diwtor Cymraeg sy'n bach o bisyn ac wi'n ffeindio'n hunan yn syllu ar ei bronnau eitha lot.
'Nes i weud bod un o'r tiwtoriaid wedi datblygu crysh bach arna i.
O'dd hi'n blêsd, os unrhywbeth.
Yn meddwl fydde'r ffaith bod rhywun arall yn 'n ffansïo yn hwb i fi.
Chwarae teg, 'naeth hi mynd trwy'r motions, yn gofyn 'She's not fitter than me, is she?'

Oh I remember that! And I said –

Ac wrth gwrs, o'dd hi'n ddigon hawdd i fi weud, No,

No way.

Not a chance.

She is no way

Not even close

Fitter than you.

Nowhere near.

And that was the truth.

Ie.

But not the whole truth.

A nid dim byd ond y gwir.

Because what I didn't mention was this girl, Lowri, had something Rachel lacked.
Lowri had desperation.
She had a terribly nice boyfriend, and they were engaged, Lowri was finishing a teaching course, and she would no doubt go on to be a teacher and have a decent career, and marriage and kids and all that.
And she was fucking desperate for something else.
It blazed off her.
I knew what that desperation meant.
I knew what it meant she would do.

'Nes i ddim sôn am hynny i Rachel, yn amlwg, d'odd e ddim yn –
– 'sda fi ddim y geiriau.

That's fucking handy.

They look at each other.

It is what it is, mate.

So I carried on having my nights out with all my friends from Welsh classes, now with Rachel's permission. I carried on not-quite flirting with Lowri, and it was all above board. I carried on pretending not to see the somewhat betrayed looks Lowri would shoot me, whenever I called time and headed home to Rachel.
One night Lowri's boyfriend turned up at the pub, obviously unasked and uninvited.
He was on at Lowri to come to the pictures with him.
Lowri was a bit pissed by then and not in the mood to sit and be quiet in the cinema.
So her boyfriend stayed. It seemed like he had a nice time. I thought I got on with him; or at least he talked to me a lot.

Corrected my Welsh a fair bit. Lowri bollocked him for that.
Apparently afterwards he laid down the law.
Said Lowri was spending too much extra-curricular time with her students.
That was obviously rubbish ’cause we only arranged a night out say once every fortnight.
So I think it was he felt a bit threatened. By me.
I found I liked being a bit of a threat.

Welais i ddim o Lowri ar ôl hynny. O’dd hi ddim yn dysgu fi ddim mwy, a fydde wastad rhyw esgus ’da hi am beidio troi lan i’n nosweithiau yn y pyb.
Clywais i tho bod hi a’i chariad wedi gwahanu cwpl o fisoedd wedyn.
Dyw rhai pethau jyst ddim yn gweithio mas.

I remember I came home from the pub that night absolutely buzzing.
Rachel was there only come in from work five minutes before.
She said, ‘I’m shattered, do you mind getting dinner?’
I said, I would cook for you love but I’m too pissed to be safe round gas and blades.
She put something together quick, just beans on toast but I made sure to show my thanks.
I said, nice one darling, stodge to soak up the booze, exactly what I need.
Rachel said
She said nothing, she said, just that she had, yeah some statements to / go over

/ Rachel said, I’ve been thinking. And what I think is, maybe you should get a fucking job.

Cheers, mate.

Hapus i helpu.

And I didn't panic.
I just put down my fork.
Wiped my mouth, and I said
Yes alright darling. Let's go for it.
I just wonder how easy it will be to get a fucking job as you put it, when people read on my CV I've suffered effectively a nervous breakdown and three years of clinical depression?
Because I want to be very honest with my prospective employer.
That's just my way.
Rachel said she appreciated the gaps in my CV would make my work-search all the more challenging, but that her idea was that I find full time voluntary work. Something that would build up my confidence. And would demonstrate I was capable of holding down a job.
I said, that sounds marvellous darling, we'll talk about it in the morning yeah?
And she said
That she had seen adverts
The local primary
Wanting local people to come in
And volunteer to help out.
Her grand plan was that I, a person of notoriously fragile temperament, should spend my days right in the den of the rat children who are going to bring down society. And not even get fucking paid for it.
I put forward my objections in as reasonable terms as I could muster.
And Rachel started to cry.
She cried and cried saying –

They look at each other – is the Welsh-speaker going to have to say this?

After everything I've done for you, after everything I've been through, after what I put up with every day to keep a roof over our heads.
Very much making it about her, when in fact it was my life that was under discussion.

Y diwrnod wedyn o'dd gyda ni noson mas, ond dim ond fi ac Andrew and Mary, y ficars priod, troeodd lan.
Ar ôl awr, symudon ni o'r bar llachar lle fydden ni'n cwrdd fel arfer, i pyb mwglyd rownd y cornel. Ac achos o'dd y pyb yn llai o faint, ac yn fwy tawel na'r bar, dechreuon ni i gyd teimlo tamaid bach yn hunan-ymwybodol yn siarad Gymraeg.
Nid jyst oherwydd y ffaith o'n ni'n siarad iaith wahanol i bawb arall – ond achos o'dd siarad Cymraeg yn amlwg yn bach o ymdrech i ni gyd.
Troeon ni at Saesneg yn y diwedd, ac am y tro cyntaf.
O'dd hi fel ddod i nabod ein gilydd unwaith 'to.
Ond nid cweit yr un pobol o'dd yn siarad nawr.
'Nes i sôn rhywfaint am . . . 'fy sefyllfa'.
Faint o gywilydd o'n i'n teimlo.
Achos wi'n credu bod cywilydd yn rhan pwysig o'r peth.
Ti'n byw mewn gwlad cyfoethog, mae gyda ti digon i fwyta, mae gyda ti rhywle i fyw, ond ti'n methu ymdopi. Wrth gwrs ti'n mynd i deimlo cywilydd.
Wedyn ti'n gorfod ymdopi gyda'r cywilydd, ar ben popeth arall.
Ac mae popeth arall yn gormod i ti eniwei, so – ti'n ffycd.
A wedodd Andrew, neu Mary, wi ddim yn cofio pa un –
"We don't see things quite the same way."

The English-speaker is immediately paying attention.

Wedon nhw
"We are all fragile."

What's that?

Wedon nhw
"Each of us will have to face things that we can't bear alone."

What, everyone?

Wedon nhw
"All of us are broken by life."

All these people here?

Wedon nhw
"And so there's no question of coping, or not coping."

None at all.

Wedon nhw
"All of us will need help from somewhere."

And where? Where does it come from?

Yr eiliad 'na, teimlais i pwysau'r cywilydd yn codi oddi wrtha i.
Cerdded adre, 'nes i ystyried yr holl fusnes o fynd mewn i'r ysgol a meddwl – pam lai? Beth yw'r peth gwaetha all digwydd?
Ac am y tro cyntaf yn 'm mywyd, 'nes i weud y frawddeg dansierus 'na wrth 'n hunan heb glwyed yr ateb 'rhyfel niwcliyr, yn amlwg' yn gefn fy meddwl.

Somehow – Christ knows how – I found the nerve.
I said yes, I would look into this classroom assistant thing.
Suddenly it was all smiles and blow jobs again.
I made the calls, filled out the disclosure forms. The police confirmed I was not a child murderer or registered paedophile, at least to the best of their knowledge.

All I had to do was give it a go, be shit – and then presumably I'd get fired. If you can fire volunteers? I don't know quite how that works.
But once I'd shown willing, and it had been proven I was useless then
I'd be safe.
We'd have to go back to the way things were.

Na, sa i'n credu bo ni'n mynd nôl.

I was given a date and on that date I presented myself to the secretary at the primary school down the road.

Ni'n mynd i ffeindio ffordd o symud ymlaen.

Full of hope.

Wi'n mynd i, eniwei.

Like a fucking idiot.

TWO

The problem was, the kids.
The kids were horrible.
Not all of them, but enough.
I don't mean they were vicious, or stupid, or rude.
They were all those things, but what I mean is, they were horrible to me.
With the teachers, mostly, they shut up and did as they were told.
With me – they knew.
They knew, and they just took the piss.
Ten, eleven year old kids, they were fucking merciless.
It was like being back in school.
At first they were calling me sir and I said no they didn't have to call me sir they could call me by my name and that was it.
What is your name, sir?
I said to them, my name is Gary and you can call me Gary you do not need to call me sir.
They said, is your name Gay-ree, sir? Is it Gay-ree? Is it Gay-boy? Is your name Gaylord, sir?
I tried to laugh it off.

He laughs.

They said,

Why are you laughing, sir? What's funny?

One of them said,

Are you mad, sir, just laughing at nothing?

I kneeled down to try and talk to this kid, person to person.

Something hit me on the back of the head. A pen, or a ruler.
I said, I certainly will be getting mad, you do anything like that again.

Another kid said,

Anything like what, sir? Did someone do something to you, sir?

And then someone tapped the back of my knee, and my leg gave way.
I turned to look at the rat child responsible.

He was smiling. He said,

What, sir? What you looking at me for, sir? Do you fancy me, sir?

I told him to fuck off.

All the kids went –

Ahhhhh, sir swore.
You swore sir.
Sir said fuck.

They got the teacher, in whose classroom I was supposed to be assisting, involved.

Miss sir said fuck.
Miss sir told Conor to fuck off.

And this little kid, Conor, got up and started out of the classroom.
The teacher said, Conor, where d'you think you're going?

Conor said –

I'm fucking off, miss. Gay-ree told me to.

At the end of the session the teacher took me aside and said,

Look, my class has been very disrupted this morning .

I said to her, yes, I was wondering when you were gonna do something about it.
She said

I'm going to do something about it right now.

She walked me down the corridor to the headmaster's office and said

I don't want you in my class this afternoon, or any afternoon, or ever. Your presence is causing far too much disruption. And that's not fair on the kids.

I sat there in the headmaster's office for a while.
I felt like – the Christian who'd been thrown to the lions, but the lions hadn't fancied eating him, and Caesar had taken that as a sign from his pagan gods and decided to let the poor bugger go.
Like I'd really been through the mill, you know?
But relieved as well 'cause I knew soon I'd be home, and safe.
The headmaster sat with me. A nice guy, actually. Much younger than he looked.
Very positive about most things.
After a while I'd collected myself and I got up and made to go.
The headmaster said

Now hold on.
There is one thing you might be able to help us with.

I said I'm not picking up crisp packets off the school field or any of that kind of nonsense.

The headmaster said

No, this is – this is something else.

He took me to a class, they had say a dozen kids, all different ages.
These kids were refugees. They were being taught English really intensively, and the ideas was then they could move off into normal classes.

Fel fi, yng Nglynderwen, neud wersi Cymraeg trwy'r bore, pob bore, er mwyn dala lan.

These refugee kids were incredible.
I don't necessarily mean that in a totally good way.
They had this dead calm about them.
And I'm sure to their families they were little . . . you know, hellraisers.
But with us –
You had to find ways to communicate with them. To connect.

Do'dd gyda nhw ddim y geiriau.

They were so quiet, and polite, and attentive –

– a diolchgar.

And I could cope with them. I could cope with dead calm.
I knew they were calm because they'd seen awful things and now very little could affect them.
But I didn't let that bother me. Didn't think too much about it.

Getting a smile out of them was a huge event.
I managed it occasionally.
By tripping over, walking into tables, dropping things.
All sorts of slapstick, they loved.
You just had to get used to the fact that if they were ecstatically happy and bursting with joy about something, on the surface that would translate into smiling about it, ever so slightly.
It was half-term and on the Friday night I was having a few drinks with Rachel while we cooked and I said I was actually not looking forward to the holiday 'cause I was gonna miss the kids because I loved them to bits.
And Rachel put down her glass, and went –

Do you realise what you just said?

And I went, what, what?
Rachel really drew it out, going –

You've really got no idea, have you?

I kept on going what, what, what, what, what, what, what, what?
For ages. Till finally she went –

You just said that you love your kids.

And I realised that I had said it: and I realised that I meant it.
A month later, one of the paid assistants left and they offered me her job.
And in the back of my mind I remember this madness telling me that once I had a job, once I was 'finished' then Rachel would leave me.
And it just seemed like what it was: madness.
Everything had changed, the moment I realised, I loved those children.

Y gwir o'dd, o'n i 'di caru'r plant 'na – ers y prynhawn cynta'. O'n i jyst yn rhy swil, neu rhy ofnus, neu rhy embarrassed i gyfadde'r peth.

You can't love something you're afraid of.

The Welsh-speaker looks at the English-speaker.

So you can't be afraid, of something you love.

The English-speaker looks back at the Welsh-speaker.

What?

Dim byd.

They're looking at each other.

Anyway –

– cachgi.

What? There's nothing to say. There is nothing, to say.

Os ti'n / gweud.

/ So here I was, a man with a job, and a girlfriend, and a social circle. I paid tax. I had become a citizen.
The mountain had been moved, a shovel-full at a time. It might not have been magic, but it was a miracle.
Rachel had saved my life.

Diwedd y stori. Ac am unwaith, mae'r stori'n dod i ben ar nodyn hapus.

After that we just lived.

Yn anffodus, er bod straeon yn dod i ben yn daclus, dyw bywydau ddim.

That madness I had suffered under – was gone. Conquered.
And it would never come back again.

Mae bywydau yn cario 'mlaen ar ôl diwedd y stori: neu mae nhw'n dod i ben cyn i'r stori cael ei gwblhau.

So thank you, thank you ladies and gentle men, thank you for sitting, listening, sharing, thanks for sticking with me right through to my triumphant victory over depression and my rehabilitation as a productive citizen who does not advocate the stoving in of children's heads, no no not one bit.
Thank you, very much.
You may leave now if you wish.

Ond nawr o'dd bywyd cyfan o'n flaen i.

What I mean is – you better had. Leave.

Bywyd allen i neud unrhywbeth o'n i'n moyn gyda fe.

Because if you don't then
You will hear me speak words which claim to represent what happened next.

Falle nid cweit unrhywbeth, ond . . .

Because next
After my happy ending
A couple of things happened at once.
First, Rachel had trouble at work.

Ac yn ail, 'naeth Lowri ymuno â'r ysgol.

It started out Rach cocked some conveyancing up, cost the firm thousands, and was all down to her being a bit slapdash, because she was bored.

'Naeth fi a Lowri osgoi ein gilydd am wythnosau, ond nos Wener o'dd criw o'r athrawon yn mynd mas. Wrth gwrs aeth Lowri, i ddod i nabod pobl.
Ac es i, achos o'n i'n moyn drinc.
Erbyn hanner 'di naw daeth fi a Lowri i fod yn eistedd yn agos at ein gilydd.
Dechrais i siarad â hi, er mwyn bod yn gwrtais.
Achos o'dd ddim o'r athrawon arall yn siarad Gymraeg, 'naeth pobol symud o gwmpas y bwrdd, yn gadael fi a Lowri yn eistedd gyda'n gilydd.

Rachel started taking time off.
Not holidays, just phoning in sick, saying she couldn't be arsed. Not when she phoned in sick, obviously: that was to me.
I'd go off to school and come home and she'd still be in her dressing gown.
I'd ask her what she'd been up to all day, she'd say 'Watching TV, masturbating, occasionally both at the same time.'
Ordinarily I might find a line like that quite arousing but coming from a girl slumped on the settee, greasy haired, with dirty dishes in the sink – it just struck me as a bit vulgar.

O'dd Lowri yn teimlo o'n i 'di bod yn annheg gyda hi.
O'n i 'di bod yn leading her on, i rhyw raddau.
Dim byd o'n i 'di gweud ond . . . y ffordd o'n i'n edrych arni hi.
Ar ei chorff.
Wedais i falle 'nes i ddim rheoli 'n hunan o'i chwmpas cystal â dylwn i fod wedi neud.
Oherwydd ei harddwch.

Wedodd hi, ti'n meddwl bo fi'n hardd, te?
Wedais i, fuck aye.

I said to Rachel that since I had some experience of being down, perhaps I could give her a few tips for getting through it?
She told me to fuck off.
I said that in a relationship people should be able to learn from one another.
She said sorry weren't you listening: I think I told you to fuck off, didn't I?
Obviously ours wasn't a relationship of equals, I never minded admitting that.
But I used to learn things from my kids, all the time.
Why shouldn't Rachel learn a thing or two from me?

Wedais i wrth Lowri, y peth yw, wi'n paranoid, neurotic mess.
Wedodd hi dwyt ti ddim.
Wedais i ydw, wi jyst yn ridiculously neurotig a needy.
Neurotig ac anghenus, wedodd Lowri, yn diwtor Cymraeg i'r diwedd. A dyna'r peth diwetha wyt ti.
Dyna'r peth ola ydw i, 'nes i feddwl. Yn dysgwr i'r diwedd.
Ond wedais i ddim hynny. Beth wedais i o'dd, wi yn . . . anghenus, a fi dylai wybod.
Wedodd Lowri, falle bo ti ddim yn nabod dy hunan cystal â ti'n meddwl. 'Swn i'n gweud bod 'na rhywbeth . . . tsen, amdanat ti.

I wouldn't let it go. I went on and on at Rachel. I said to her –

Tsen?

Do you see sometimes a bloke who just bloody gets things done – a barrister, a police sergeant, a criminal element – and think you'd prefer to be with a man like that?

Tsen?

That it would be easier to be with a man like that?

Tsen?

That your life might have turned out different, and by different what I mean is better, if you were with a man like that?

Tsen?

I said, I only ask you these things because the truth, even really brutal truth, psychologists guarantee is easier to cope with than doubt.

Am ages o'n i'n styc, yn methu ffigro mas beth o'dd y peth 'tsen' o'dd Lowri'n cyhuddo fi o fod.
A wedyn sylweddolais i. O'n i 'di cymryd bod hi 'di gweud gair yn dechrau gyda'r sŵn 'ts', sy'n mynd yn lle 'jay', pan ma' pobol yn fod yn offensively gywir ac yn mynnu gweud er enghraifft 'garets' yn lle 'garej'.
Ond beth o'dd hi 'di gweud o'dd rhywbeth yn dechrau gyda 'zed'.
Zed Eee Enn.
O'dd Lowri 'di gweud bod 'na rhywbeth 'Zen'.
Amdani i.

It took her ages. She cried and cried.
I found I was able to sit through all the tears, quite calmly.
In the end, Rachel admitted that yes.
Sometimes she imagined being with a man who –
That it might be easier if –
That sexually it was sometimes difficult to –
But she felt these things only occasionally.
She was only admitting to them to be honest.
Because I had requested honesty.
I said thank you that's a great help.
A very great help indeed.

Ar ôl i fi stopio chwerthin, wedais i – what the fuck?
Wedodd Lowri, na, o ddifri. Mae 'na rhywbeth Zen amdanat ti. Ti ddim yn gweud lot, a pan ti yn gweud rhywbeth, mae'n rhywbeth rîli syml, sy'n dod syth at y pwynt.
A ti ddim yn neud lot, ond pan ti yn neud rhywbeth, dwyt ti ddim yn trafod am ages neu becso am os wyt ti'n neud y peth iawn. Ti jyst yn neud be' sydd ishe neud.
Gyda rhai pobol sy'n eitha tawel, ti'n cael yr argraff bod loads yn mynd ymlaen yn ei meddwl. Ond ti ddim fel 'na. Ti'n rhoi'r argraff bod dy feddwl yn dawel, hefyd.
Triais i egluro iddi hi y pethau o'dd yn mynd ymlaen yn fy meddwl, trwy'r amser. Y pethau dwl, hunanol, creulon, paranoid, neurotig, anghenus. 'Nes i dreial rhoi enghreifftiau –
– ond o'n i'n methu.
O'dd 'da fi ddim y geiriau.
Achos o'dd fi a Lowri wastad yn siarad Gymraeg 'da'n gilydd. O rhyw fath.

Getting the truth out of Rachel was a real weight off.
Because it made clear my situation was not sustainable.

Mae 'na rhywbeth dyw e ddim yn gweud 'tha chi.
A mewn ffordd dyw e ddim 'n lle i i weud, os ma' fe 'di penderfynu beidio.
Ond wi ddim yn siwr bod e wedi neud penderfyniad clir am y peth.
Weithiau ma' fe'n anghofio'r manylyn bach yma.
Amazing i feddwl bod pobl yn gallu anghofio pethau fel hyn, ond – mae'n digwydd.
Neu bod e jyst yn rhy embarrassed.

Walking into class the next day, I turned down a corridor.
I saw one of my kids – a little Kurdish girl – and two boys from year seven.

The first boy standing behind my little girl, holding her arms.
The second boy was in front of her. One hand over her mouth.
The other hand –
– I'd say rubbing her breasts but she didn't have any, she was only eight.
So what he was doing, was rubbing the places on her chest where breasts would one day develop.
The tears in her eyes were not fear, or shock.
They were tears of exhaustion.
All three of them heard me coming, and turned to look.
The kid who was holding the girl, shat himself.
The girl – in a split-second, her eyes filled with triumph.
And the ratboy actually committing the sexual assault.
He smiled.
What his smile told me was, that he knew he would get away with this.
It would be his word, and his mate's word, against the girl's.
It would be his parents, against hers.
His parents would be loud and aggressive and would make trouble for the school.
Whereas hers were of dubious legal status and probably couldn't speak English.
And in the ratboy's smile I saw
Exactly how my situation would cease to sustain.
All I had to do was
Break the nasty little ratty jaw
And that would be it.

Mae Rachel yn bwrw fe.
Nid pob dydd, dim byd rîli ddifrifol, ond weithiau – pan mae hi'n feddw.
Neu pan mae hi'n rîli grac.
Sa i'n gweud mae bod e'r un peth pan mae merch yn bwrw dyn a pan mae dyn yn bwrw merch.
Achos dyw e ddim.

Fuodd e byth mewn ofn am ei fywyd, fuodd e byth mewn ofn cael lôs difrifol.
Falle dyna pam mae fe'n dioddef y peth – achos, mewn ffordd, dyw e ddim yn rhywbeth difrifol.
Hefyd – wel, mae fe'n demanding neurotic mess, mae hi'n bwrw fe bob hyn a hyn.
Rhaid cael give and take mewn pob perthynas.

I had never hit anyone before in my life, at this point.
But I knew that I could hit him.
And because he was so much smaller than me
I knew I'd do some serious damage.
Enough that he wouldn't get up again, and have a go back.
Enough that his ratboy friend would be frightened and run away.
Enough that my little girl would see
That evil is punished in this world, and innocence, occasionally, defended.

Mae e'n treial edrych ar y peth fel problem dim ond i Rachel.
Rhywbeth fydd rhaid i hi sortio mas.
Rhywbeth sydd ddim rîli yn effeithio arno fe.
Ond – yn amlwg – mae yn effeithio arno fe.
Achos mae'n dangos iddo fe
Bod Rachel yn ei gasáu e.
Otherwise how come mae hi'n bwrw fe?

– and then I thought of what would happen.
There'd be a confrontation with his parents.
Probably outside our house.
There'd be loads of them. A mob.
I'd lose my temper. That would be embarrassing.
Because the mob would lose their tempers too, and their tempers would be worse.
There'd be violence.

The police called. If I was lucky.
When the police came they'd take one look at this – angry mob, and one look at me, and they'd know who the troublemaker was.
The loner. Obviously.
And as it became clear that I was able to answer questions in complete sentences, the initial suspicions of the officers would be confirmed.
And Jesus God what would happen to me in the cells.
The twin Stanley blades fixed to a toothbrush.
A parallel cut, that can't be stitched.

Felly mae'r person sy'n byw gyda fe, sy'n cysgu 'da fe, sy'n gofalu amdano fe, sy'n bwydo fe, sy'n neud e chwerthin, sy'n chwarae gyda fe, sy'n ffycio fe, sy' wedi gwella fe
– y person sy'n nabod e'n well na neb –
mae hi yn ei gasáu e.
It's hardly a good sign.

That's what we do to scum who hit kiddies.

O'dd e fel eiliad 'naeth para am flwyddyn.

It was like a second that lasted for a year.

Fi, y ferch, y bechgyn ffiaidd –

Me, the girl, the rat boys –

Yr un bachgen yn cachu'i hunan. Y bachgen arall yn gwenu.

One of the boys shitting himself, the other boy smiling.

A 'nes i jyst anadlu.

I just breathed,

Mewn, mas.

In, out –

Fy meddwl, am unwaith, yn hollol ddistaw.

My hand found the shape of a fist.

A 'nes i fwrw'r bastad.
Aeth e yn erbyn y wal, a syth lawr.
Gwaed yn llifo o'i drwyn.
Dant bach melyn ar y llawr.
Y boi arall yn sefyll, ei geg ar agor.
Y ferch yn chwerthin.

And then I let my fist go limp.
I told the boys to go to the headmaster's office.
They laughed. Both of them smiling now.
They sauntered off. Not in the direction of the headmaster's, but I couldn't say anything 'cause I had temporarily lost my voice.
I turned to the girl, and tried to speak.
Which was foolish of me because I'd only realised that second past that my voice had gone.
She was crying again now.
Crying 'cause she was eight years old, and over-tired.

Wedyn cododd y bachgen, a neidio arna i.
'Naeth e treial cnoi clust fi off, ond wrth gwrs o'n i 'di bwrw fe yn y geg, a wedi neud niwed i'w dannedd, so 'naeth e brifo ei hunan wrth neud.
'Nes i wthio fe off, ac aeth e lawr unwaith 'to.
Cododd e ddim y tro 'ma.
'Naeth neb symud o gwbl.
O'n nhw i gyd, y bechgyn a'r ferch, yn edrych tu ôl i fi.
Troeais i rownd.

A gwelais i'r prifathro yn sefyll 'na.

I walked away.
I walked away, and I went home.

Saethodd y prifathro at y boi, a pigo fe lan, a gweiddi arno fe – that's it, you little shit, I've got you now.
Achos o'dd e ddim 'di gweld fi'n bwrw'r bastad.
O'dd e 'di gweld y bastad yn neidio arna i – y classroom assistant tawel a chydwybodol – a cnoi ar 'n glust; ac o'dd e wedi cymryd taw dyna o'dd cychwyn y trais.
Fel fydde unrhyw berson gall.
O'n i'n mynd i gael getawê 'da bwrw'r bastad, ac o'dd y bastad yn mynd i gael ei ecscliwdio o'r ysgol.
Es i draw at y ferch.
Taflodd hi ei breichiau o 'n gwmpas.
Yn gweud thank you, thank you, thank you.
Ac o'n i'n gwbod o'n i 'di neud y peth iawn am unwaith.
Edrychais i lan.
A trwy'r ffenest.
A tu fas, yn eistedd ar gadair bach mewn gardd llysiau'r plant, o'dd Lowri.
Yn amlwg wedi stopio i gael sigarét slei ar ei ffordd i'r wers nesaf.
Y sigarét yn ei llaw, wedi'i llosgi reit lawr i'r styb.

I went home, and I had a long talk with Rachel.
She was still spending her days slumped on the settee, masturbating to Home and Away.
I told her how I'd been faking it for a while now.
I'd been feeling pretty bad myself, but covering it up. Trying to be strong, for her.
Little tots of vodka before I left the house. A pair of doubles in the pub for lunch.
I didn't have a drink problem per se, but I certainly was misusing drink, to get me through the day.

Rachel said she didn't believe me.
She thought I was fine.
She thought I just didn't want to cope.
How can you not want to cope?
I said it was typical for a depressed person – for example, her – to be so wrapped up in themselves they didn't notice what others – for example, me – were going through.
And I should know. Having, of the both of us, the most experience of depression.

Diwedd y dydd, o'dd Lowri yn aros amdana i.
Wedodd hi, wi'n meddwl bod rhaid i ni drafod yr hyn a ddigwyddodd heddi.
Aethon ni i'r pyb. Nid yr un lle mae'r athrawon i gyd yn mynd. Rhywle tawelach.
'Naeth un o'r assistants arall gweld fi a Lowri yn mynd off gyda'n gilydd.
Rhoeodd e wên bach i fi.
Ond d'odd Lowri ddim yn gwenu.

Rachel and I had a long talk about how we'd get by if neither of us was really fit to work.
I said I was going to go to the doctor, get anti-depressants and get signed off on the sick.
Rachel said she would try and pull herself together but she wasn't sure she could manage it.
She was worried how we'd keep up the mortgage on her mum's house.
She said it was probably best we sell up rather than let the place be repossessed.
We could rent a place but that'd cost loads, and people never want to take DSS.
We could go to a housing association but we'd hardly be a priority.
Us being a couple.

With no children.

Aeth Lowri i'r bar. Daeth hi nôl gyda'r drincs ac eistedd.
Ac o'dd rhyw lais fach yn fy mhen yn gweud dylwn i ddim fod yn y pyb gyda Lowri, dylwn i fod adre gyda Rachel.
'Nes i adael i'r llais cario 'mlaen, nes bod y geiriau ddim yn neud sens fel geiriau dim mwy, nes i'r llais troi yn sŵn, nes i sŵn y llais mynd ar goll yn sŵn fy nghorff, gwaed ac anadl, sŵn y pyb, sŵn y dre a'r byd tu fas, nes i sŵn y llais diflannu yn gyfan gwbl, nes i'n meddwl i fynd yn hollol ddistaw.

Rachel was trying to explain exactly how it'd be good for us two self-confessed depressives if we had a kid.
But then a drunken bitch chose right outside our house to stop, and shout up the street – Andrew, you black bastard, I'm gonna tell your girlfriend you've been trying to shag me the last three months.
Some bloke in one of the houses opposite politely asked her to keep the noise and the racism down to a reasonable level.
The drunken bitch carried on screaming at Andrew for another couple of minutes and then let the bloke in the house opposite know she was gonna have him fucked up, bad.
Then she wandered off back to whatever hellhole she lived in.
Me and Rachel smiled at each other.
That sort of, what can you do? smile, that decent people give each other sometimes, when the future makes itself apparent.

Wedodd Lowri bod hi 'di bod mewn i weld y prifathro y prynhawn 'na, a gweud wrtho fe beth o'dd hi 'di gweld.
Sef, fi yn cyrraedd, a gweld y bechgyn yn ymosod ar y ferch, a gweiddi arnyn nhw am stopio.
Ac wedyn welodd hi'r bastad yn neidio arna i, a cnoi 'n glust.
Ac wedyn welodd hi fi'n gwthio'r bastad off.
Ac wedyn welodd hi'r bastad yn curo'r wal, ac felly yn brifo ei drwyn a'i dannedd.

Welodd hi fi'n neud dim byd, ond amddiffyn 'n hunan.
Yn sicr, do'dd hi ddim 'di gweld fi'n bwrw'r ratboy, fel o'dd e'n honni.
Ac wedyn – 'naethon nhw galw last orders.
Ac wedodd Lowri – ti ishe dod nôl i'n lle i?
Wedais i – pam lai?

Rachel went on talking about how a kid could be the making of us.
It would settle things because – once you have a kid, you're tied to life.
Whether you want to be or not.

O'n ni 'di colli'r trêns i gyd, ac o'dd Lowri yn rhy pissed i yrru so fflagiodd hi lawr tacsi a gweud, how much to Cardiff Bay?
Wedodd y boi, forty quid?
Cymerodd y trip rhyw hanner awr. Ar y ffordd, wedon ni ddim byd.
Yn fy meddwl o'dd y llais yn sgrechan, dylwn i fod yn meddwl am Rachel, o'dd Rachel yn angen fi.
Edrychais i fewn i'n meddwl.
Ffeindio'r fro lle o'dd y llais ma'n byw.
A'i dorri mas.
'Nes i weindio ffenest y drws lawr.
Twlu'r llais mas o'r car.
Wylio fe'n bownsio ar wyneb y M4.
Diflannu o dan olwynion un o loris Oriel Jones a'i Fab Llanybydder.
Ac er o'n i wedi torri, yn nawr o'n i'n gyflawn.
Ac 'nes i jyst ishte 'na am weddill y siwrnai.
Yn edrych ar Lowri bob hyn a hyn.
Yn edrych ar siâp ei chorff.
Yn meddwl
Dim byd.

The next morning I got up, showered, dressed.
Rachel said, you off to work darling?
I said of course darling, yes.

Aethon ni lan i'w fflat hi, a jyst ffycio'n syth.
'Nes i rîli, rîli fwynhau.

The Welsh-speaker begins to move to the highest place he can reach.

Then I walked to Glanrhyd, a hospital providing a range of in-patient mental health facilities on the outskirts of Bridgend, and I made a request to be admitted.
They said I had to be referred by a doctor, and I should go and see my GP.
I knew this of course.
But I wouldn't leave.

The English-speaker begins to move to the highest place he can reach.

'Nes i gael hi unwaith yn y missionary, jyst i dwymo lan.

Really I just wanted to go there and have a look at a mental hospital and see what the people were like.
I saw some of them, being walked round the gardens.
Very obviously they were just bloody crackers.
They had delusions, they heard voices, they were obsessive and incoherent.
Whereas I –

Unwaith gyda hi ar dop, i fi cael mwynhau'r view.

– I can just see where the world's going, and I can't fucking take it.

I sat there, on a bench by the main entrance, laughing.
And I was still laughing – tears of relief, now, rolling down my cheeks – when a doctor came up, and said they'd decided to take me in for assessment.
I said but honestly, there's no need, I'm fine.

Unwaith o tu ôl, i ddangos iddi pwy sydd in charge yn y sefyllfa.

The doctor said, well why don't we talk about that inside.
So I went with him.
We talked for a long time and I said you know actually I think I do need a bit of rest.
But there wasn't much rest to be had, because the place was full of mad people who screamed at the walls, and cut themselves.

Ac unwaith yn sefyll lan, ei gwyneb yn cnocio yn erbyn y wal, jyst i neud y pwynt yn hollol glir.

In the morning Rachel came and they set me up with an appointment for my GP, and a week's worth of tranquillisers.
I said I was feeling much better.
And – that's true, I was.
Because I knew that at least I wouldn't end up with the mad people.

Ar ôl i ni bennu, mae hi'n gweud nest ti brifo fi tamaid bach y tro diwetha.
Ac yn fy meddwl i, mae 'na dim byd.
Felly wi'n gweud dim byd.
Ac yn y diwedd er mwyn llenwi'r distawrwydd mae Lowri'n gweud, 'nes i joio, tho, paid becso.

I sat at home for a bit and then one day Rachel said she was feeling better and she went out to the shops and once she was gone I thought I'd see if I could manage a walk.

I did manage. I walked for miles.
All the way to Southerndown.
I was fine going there, but then once I got to the cliffs I found I was crying.
I got a bit frustrated with myself ’cause I thought, what are you crying for now?
I knew I needed some kind of help from somewhere so I pulled out my phone.
The woman said, how would things have to change, for your life to be worth living?
My life’s not the problem. It’s everything. It’s the world. It’s the end of civilisation.
She said, but you’re the one on top of a cliff.
I said that’s right, full marks, you’ve been paying attention.
I said will you stay with me till the end.
She said she would.
But I didn’t believe that.
I said no you won’t, you liar.
And I knew I wouldn’t be able to bear it, the moment when she lied and let me down and left me there, abandoned and alone, and so I just ended the call.
Soon as I did that the phone beeped and there was a message from Rachel saying I don’t care what you’ve done, it doesn’t matter, nothing matters, just get home here or please just let me know you’re safe.
But I knew she hated me so I just deleted it and didn’t call her back.
And then a car pulled in – some desperate dad trying to restrain a toddler. The window was open and I could hear a voice I recognised. Offering up a prayer.
It was Mary.
The married vicar.
Speaking directly to me, via the medium of Radio 4’s controversial Prayer for the Day feature.
I picked up my phone and looked at it and thought

If Mary rings me now, that'll be a miracle.
And through a miracle I might be saved.
But my phone stayed still and silent.

Aethon ni i'r gwely. I gysgu.
Daeth cwsg i fi, o fewn munudau.

Then it occurred to me maybe I was asking a bit much to have
Mary phone me out of the blue that very second.
It would be a miracle, yeah – but an obvious one. A bit showy.
The kind we don't go in for anymore.
Because actually I had her number, and I could in fact phone
her.
And I thought about
Calling out to Mary
'Cause maybe she could find, Christ knows where
The strength
The patience
The love
To help me.
And I opened my phone book
Brought up her name
And it would take
Almost nothing from me
To press the call button, but then
I'd have to tell her
All these thoughts,
All these awful things,
And then, she would know me.
See like you all know me now and
It's so fucking shaming I can hardly bear it

Mae Lowri yn deffro am eiliad. Mae hi'n gweud, mae hyn yn
teimlo mor ddiniwed.
Wi'n ateb – mae'n rhodd ni'n rhannu 'da'n gilydd.

Ac mae hi'n gwenu.

I throw the phone over the edge
I see it sail down,
Smash on the rock.
A man on the beach, a tiny figure,
Looks up, starts shaking his fist at me.
All I have to face is that feeling everybody knows
From falling asleep: the sudden rush,
The stomach flipping, the heart in the mouth,
Then the relief when we come awake and realise
We are safe.
All I have to do
Is take a few steps
And I can come awake from the dream.

Ar ôl cysgu am gwpl o oriau, wi'n codi a mynd mewn i'r gegin i ôl ddŵr.
Wi'n mynd mas i'r balconi, i checio fy ffôn.
Mae 'na neges oddi wrth Rachel, yn gweud – I don't care what you've done, it doesn't matter, nothing matters, just get home here or please just let me know you're safe.
Tra gwrando a'r y neges, wi'n teimlo awel y nos ar 'n nghroen, ac yn meddwl – dim byd.

I give you one last chance, to intervene.
All my senses working overtime, seeking out
Even the slightest offer of help or hope.

Wi'n edrych lawr.

I listen for an answer, and there is

Mae 'na bobol dal o gwmpas, yn symud rhwng bars a clybs y Bae.

The wind, whipping air from my lungs.

Lluoedd ohonyn nhw.

The sea, grinding down the shore.

Ond mae nhw i gyd mor fach.

Kids on the beach, taking sides and falling out.

Mae nhw'n gweiddi a sgrechan –

A gang with bin bags and gardening gloves, tottering between rock pools, picking up twisted plastic and tied-off rubber.

– ond erbyn iddo fe cyrraedd 'nghlustiau i, mae'r sŵn wedi troi yn sibrwd, yn ymuno â sibrwd yr awel, a sibrwd y môr.

There are shoals, wheeling and surging near the sea's surface. Jellies thicken the broth further down. Whole ecologies, toxic to our own, crowd round cracks in the sea bed.
There are factory ships dredging the water for flesh, putting the bodies on ice, gutting it, packing it, sealing it in protective atmospheres.
There are stations and satellites above us. Orbiters and rovers surveying far-off planets. Probes drifting into even deeper space, their metal limbs vaporising, atom by atom into the vacuum.
There is a universe, looking for all the world like it's full of life and wonder.
Jyst sibrydion fach. Dim byd – sy'n fygythiol.

And nothing,

Popeth yn cysuro fi, rhywsut.

No-one coming to help me.

Mae Lowri'n dod mas i'r balconi.

I see the rocks below

Mae hi'n noeth, heblaw am groes auraidd yn hongian rhwng ei bronnau.

Which will break my body,

Mae hi'n sefyll nesa i fi, gyda'i phen ar fy ysgwydd.

Like the careless world has broken my Welsh heart.

Mae holl drafferthion y dinas yn pethau fach, all fyth trafferthu ni.

Shall I go on?

Yn sydyn mae'n taro fi –

I can't.

– alla i fyw fel hyn.